EAT
YOURSELF
CALM

EAT
YOURSELF
CALM

INGREDIENTS & RECIPES
TO REDUCE THE STRESS IN YOUR LIFE

GILL PAUL
NUTRITIONIST: KAREN SULLIVAN, ASET, VTCT, BSC

hamlyn

An Hachette UK Company
www.hachette.co.uk

First published in Great Britain in 2014 by Hamlyn,
a division of Octopus Publishing Group Ltd
Carmelite House
50 Victoria Embankment
London EC4Y 0DZ
www.octopusbooksusa.com

Distributed in the US by Hachette Book Group,
1290 Avenue of the Americas, 4th and 5th Floors
New York, NY 10020

Distributed in Canada by Canadian Manda Group,
664 Annette Street, Toronto, Ontario,
Canada M6S 2C8

Copyright © Octopus Publishing Group Ltd 2014

ISBN 978-0-600-62703-6

A CIP catalog record for this book is available from
the Library of Congress.

Printed and bound in China

10 9 8 7 6

All reasonable care has been taken in the
preparation of this book but the information
it contains is not intended to take the place of
treatment by a qualified medical practitioner.

People with known nut allergies should avoid
recipes containing nuts or nut derivatives,
and vulnerable people should avoid dishes
containing raw or lightly cooked eggs.

Standard level kitchen spoon and cup
measurements are used in all recipes.

Ovens should be preheated to the specified
temperature—if using a convection oven,
follow the manufacturer's instructions for adjusting
the time and temperature. Medium eggs should be
used unless otherwise stated.

Some of the recipes in this book have previously
appeared in other titles published by Hamlyn.

Art Director: Jonathan Christie
Photographic Art Direction and Prop Styling:
Isabel de Cordova
Photography: Will Heap
Food Styling: Joy Skipper
Editors: Katy Denny & Alex Stetter
Copy Editor: Jo Smith
Assistant Production Manager: Caroline Alberti

CONTENTS

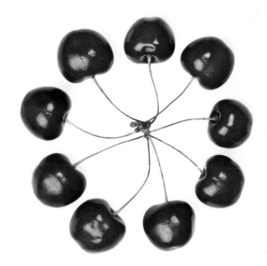

INTRODUCTION

Modern life is full of challenges and we all get stressed from time to time. We are pulled in different directions as we balance the demands of work and family, juggle our finances, keep up with the housework, and cope with the daily commute. Our bodies are designed to cope with some short-term stress, but when it continues over weeks and months, it can cause physical, mental, and emotional problems. These problems make us feel tired, depressed, and unwell—and even more stressed.

Of course, we need to address the sources of our stress, but this may involve life changes that we can't achieve overnight. There is, however, one change that works instantly—taking control of what we eat and drink. By choosing the right foods, we can get our bodies back to a place of calm, so that both physically and emotionally we are much better equipped to deal with whatever life has in store. There are loads of delicious, nutritious foods that positively support all the body systems during periods of stress and target the symptoms that accompany stress. We can literally eat ourselves calm.

The science of stress

The body's initial reaction to stress is known as the "fight or flight" response, because it provides the rush of energy we might need to confront or run away from a dangerous situation. Our brains trigger the release of the hormones adrenaline, noradrenaline, and cortisol, which speed up the heart and breathing rates. Blood is diverted away from the digestive system, skin, and organs, such as the kidneys, and sent to the muscles, where it might be needed to take physical action. The mouth will feel dry, we may sweat more, our hearts are racing—but we can deal with the stress.

If the stressful situation continues, different hormones swing into action to increase our blood sugar levels, giving us prolonged energy, and raising our blood pressure to help us maintain circulation. We can manage like this for a while, but if we remain stressed over a long period, the body becomes exhausted because so many of its systems are being forced to overwork, while vital organs are being deprived of the nutrients they need for healthy function.

In short, our bodies are designed to cope with short bursts of stress caused by physical threat; they are ill-equipped to deal with the long-term mental and emotional stresses that we often experience in the modern world.

The long-term effects of stress

- Prolonged high levels of the stress hormone cortisol depress the immune system, so we are more susceptible to catch any bugs going around.
- Blood sugar levels fluctuate, affecting energy levels and mood.
- If blood pressure is high for too long, it causes changes in the arteries, which means blood pressure doesn't drop again even when the stress has passed.
- Stress leads to raised levels of cholesterol in the blood, which is linked to heart and circulatory disease.

- The digestive system becomes sluggish, inflamed, and prone to cramps and bloating. It has trouble absorbing the nutrients in our food.
- Cortisol makes us lay down fat around our waists, which is linked to heart disorders.
- We sleep badly, which means the body doesn't have time to recharge.
- All of this plays havoc with hormones and brain function, causing a host of emotional symptoms, such as anxiety, depression, and mood swings.

How to eat yourself calm

1. Keep blood sugar levels steady

When you are very stressed, you may find you get cravings for fatty, sugary foods. These give a quick hit of energy, but soon after eating them your blood sugar will dip and you'll feel even more sluggish than before. One of the keys to dealing with stress is to keep your blood sugar as steady as possible, and that means eating regular small snacks and meals throughout the day, comprising foods that the body will burn at a slow, steady rate.

The glycemic Index rates foods according to their effect on blood sugar. High-GI foods, such as sugary drinks, white bread, and candies, are broken down quickly by the digestive system and cause blood sugar to soar, then plummet. Low-GI foods, such as vegetables and beans, produce a slow, steady release of energy. These are the foods to choose.

2. Top up the B vitamins

A range of vitamins and minerals containing different antioxidants and phytonutrients are essential for good health. But during stressful periods, the B group vitamins are especially useful, because they support the nervous system and brain function and stimulate the production of feel-good hormones, such as serotonin. The B vitamins can become depleted when we are stressed, making us anxious and depressed, so it's vital to top them up—and eating whole grains, mushrooms, oily fish, poultry, nuts, vegetables, and beans is the best way.

3. Eat a lot of antioxidants

Antioxidant vitamins A, C, and E are also crucial to boost the immune system and protect the body from the damaging effects of long-term stress. They help to lower blood pressure, protect the heart and digestive system, and encourage brain function. Opt for fruits and vegetables with the brightest colors, because these are the ones with the highest antioxidant levels.

4. Look after your digestive system

There are several ways to support your digestive system: eat plenty of fiber-rich foods to prevent constipation, drink loads of water to flush it all through, and include plenty of yogurt with live cultures in your diet to boost levels of healthy bacteria in your digestion. Junk foods, such as burgers, pizzas, and fried foods, give the digestive system a heavy load, so avoid them while your system is under strain.

5. Promote restful sleep

Getting a good night's sleep makes everything look better the next day, and it is also essential for regulating hormones, maintaining healthy blood pressure, balancing mood, improving energy levels, and keeping a strong immune system. Calcium, magnesium, and certain amino acids aid restful sleep and you'll find them in abundance in the recipes in this book.

6. Reduce caffeine and alcohol

Caffeine is a stimulant and produces many of the same effects on the body as stress hormones, so when you are trying to reduce stress, it makes sense to stick to one or two cups of coffee a day, and avoid caffeine in the evenings. Alcohol is a depressant and, while you won't have refreshing sleep after drinking a lot, one glass of red wine from time to time can have health benefits from the antioxidants it contains.

Achieving inner calm

The moment you start eating stress-reducing foods, you will feel the benefits. Your energy, mood, and concentration will improve, and gradually the niggling symptoms of stress will disappear. Meanwhile, your internal organs will be functioning more healthily, so you will be less prone to infections and long-term life-threatening disease. Follow the meal planner on pages 30–33, or use the problem solver on pages 26–29 to identify the key ingredients that will address your specific symptoms. Find them in the section on superfoods, pages 12–25, to discover how you can include them in your meals.

Of course, diet alone won't solve everything that may be problematic in your life. If you have a tyrannical boss, a hectic work- and home-life schedule, credit card meltdown, or a leaking roof, improving your diet won't take these issues away—but it will make you feel calmer and give you the energy you need to take them on. Your energy and focus will improve, and the niggling symptoms that have blighted your life will disappear. You'll be able to deal with problems more effectively, thereby reducing stress even farther. So to achieve that win–win situation, this book is the perfect guide.

CALM
SUPERFOODS

SUPERFOODS

These functional foods support your health on all levels and offer long-term protection against high blood pressure and other stress-related conditions.

Dark chocolate

- ✔ Lowers blood pressure and cholesterol
- ✔ Balances blood sugar
- ✔ Reduces stress hormones
- ✔ Lifts mood
- ✔ Boosts energy

Eating just 1½ oz of dark chocolate every day lowers levels of the stress hormone cortisol, as well as the "fight or flight" hormones released by our adrenal glands when we are under pressure. Choose bars with at least 70 percent cocoa solids.

It's rich in ...

- → Antioxidants, which boost immunity and encourage heart health
- → Phenethylamine, a natural ingredient that is released in the brain when we experience positive emotions
- → Oleic acid, a cholesterol-busting fat
- → Magnesium, which eases headaches, fatigue, and palpitations
- → Iron, helping to even mood, ease headaches, and boost energy

Use in ... sauces and stews; grate onto fresh fruit or yogurt; snack on a handful of chocolate-covered brazil nuts, or just nibble a couple of small squares as an after-dinner treat. But remember: chocolate does contain sugar and fat, and can play havoc with weight and blood sugar levels.

SEE: CHOCOLATE & ALMOND SQUARES, P. 63; DARK CHOCOLATE FONDUE WITH FRUIT & NUTS, P. 122; SOUR CHERRY CHOCOLATE BROWNIE CAKES, P. 124.

Mango

✔ Regulates blood pressure
✔ Reduces stress hormones
✔ Boosts immunity
✔ Improves memory
✔ Eases digestion

The bright orange flesh of a single ripe mango contains more than three times the vitamin C of a glass of orange juice, and it has been shown to regulate stress hormones and blood pressure. Rich in iron, mango will also improve energy levels.

It's rich in ...
→ Antioxidants and phenols, which protect against heart disease and stroke
→ Prebiotics and fiber, which encourage healthy digestion
→ Potassium, helping to ease palpitations and lower blood pressure
→ Vitamin C, good for immunity, heart, eyes, and skin
→ Vitamin B_6, helpful for relaxation, stress reduction, and increased energy

Use in ... salads with feta cheese, chicken, and pecans; top with mascarpone cheese, honey, and cinnamon and grill until bubbling; blend with raspberries and/or yogurt for an instant, stress-busting breakfast; toss into curries and stews; or eat fresh and ripe.

SEE: APRICOT, MANGO & PINEAPPLE SMOOTHIE, P. 62; FRUITY MANGO OAT BARS, P. 64; GINGERED TOFU & MANGO SALAD, P. 80; FISH & MANGO CURRY WITH BROWN RICE, P. 88; MANGO BRÛLÉE, P. 108.

Oats

✔ Support the nervous system
✔ Lift energy levels and relieve fatigue
✔ Encourage healthy digestion
✔ Promote restful sleep

Oats have long been recognized for their positive impact on the nervous system and, when eaten regularly, have been shown to reduce the effects of stress and relieve fatigue. Oats soothe the digestive system and contain a lot of protein to encourage overall health and to help stabilize blood sugar and energy levels.

They are rich in ...
→ Soluble fiber, helping to lower blood cholesterol and aid digestion
→ The B vitamins, stimulating the production of the feel-good hormone serotonin
→ Calcium, potassium, and vitamin A, essential for a healthy nervous system
→ Magnesium, which counters irritability and anxiety, and soothes headaches
→ Slow-release carbohydrates, which provide long-term energy
→ Phytonutrients (plant chemicals), which protect the body from chronic diseases such as cancer and heart disease

Use in ... oatmeal, or sprinkle on cereals, yogurt, and fruit; add oats to your fruit crisp toppings and snack on oat bars to keep energy levels high. Throw a handful into soups, stews, and casseroles, and make a savory crumb topping for a fish casserole.

SEE: APPLE & YOGURT MUESLI, P. 36; BLUEBERRY & OAT MUFFINS, P. 40; BREAKFAST CEREAL BARS, P. 43.

Salmon

✔ Supports the nervous system
✔ Eases inflammation
✔ Aids memory and concentration
✔ Lifts mood

Salmon is rich in the important B vitamins that fight stress, encourage a healthy nervous system, and help produce the happy brain chemical serotonin. The omega oils it contains have been shown to reduce levels of adrenaline and other stress hormones.

It's rich in ...

→ Omega oils, which ease inflammation, improve brain function, and reduce the risk of heart disease and stroke
→ DHA (docosahexaenoic acid), known to reduce depression and improve mood and cognition
→ Selenium, for healthy heart and joints
→ Vitamins B_6 and B_{12}, reducing the emotional and physical effects of stress
→ Vitamin D and certain proteins that reduce inflammation causing headaches and other aches and pains

Use in ... scrambled eggs for a high-protein, stress-busting breakfast; toss flakes into pasta dishes, risottos, and herb salads; or serve on rye bread with light mayonnaise and a little chopped dill. Poach and top with a scraping of pesto; roast in the oven with fresh asparagus; or make into fish cakes or burgers.

SEE: HERBED SMOKED SALMON OMELET, P. 48; SALMON & ASPARAGUS ROLL UPS, P. 50; GREEN LENTILS WITH FLAKED SALMON, P. 72; SALMON WITH MASHED BEANS & CELERIAC, P. 90.

Ginger

✔ Eases digestive complaints
✔ Reduces muscle pain and inflammation
✔ Improves mood
✔ Encourages the absorption of nutrients

Numerous studies have shown the impact of ginger on symptoms of stress. It boosts libido and mood, acts as an analgesic for headaches and muscle pain, and settles a stressed digestive system. It's also rich in nutrients that encourage immunity and ease the impact of stress hormones on the nervous system.

It's rich in ...

→ Gingerol, a phytonutrient that has been shown to reduce muscle pain by 25 percent, ease tension-related headaches, improve digestion by stimulating taste buds and saliva, and reduce nausea
→ Antioxidants, helping to boost the immune system
→ Vitamin B_6, to protect against the emotional and physical effects of stress
→ Chemicals that protect the brain from unhealthy blood sugar levels, which can be caused by prolonged stress

Use in ... hot lemon and ginger tea; grate into curries and soups for extra warming zest; add to stir-fries and stir into fruit salads; mix with honey and use to flavor plain yogurt with live cultures.

SEE: GINGERED TOFU & MANGO SALAD, P. 80; THAI MUSSEL CURRY WITH GINGER, P. 92; ROOT VEGETABLE STEW WITH POMEGRANATE SALSA, P. 94; GINGERY CHICKPEA CURRY, P. 96.

Turkey

✔ Encourages restful sleep
✔ Reduces anxiety
✔ Lifts mood
✔ Regulates nervous system function

The amino acids contained in turkey not only promote a feeling of calm and even sleepiness, but they are also responsible for improving mood and regulating your sleep cycle. Low in saturated fats, it's a healthy alternative to many types of meat, and the B vitamins it contains help the body to process fats, thus easing digestion.

It's rich in ...

→ Tryptophan, encouraging the release of the feel-good chemical serotonin, which lifts mood and aids sleep
→ Phenylalanine, an amino acid that helps to prevent depression
→ Vitamins B_3 and B_6, to support the nervous system. They become depleted in times of stress
→ Selenium, helping to promote the healthy function of the immune system
→ Protein, balancing blood sugar and providing amino acids to aid tissue repair

Use in ... crunchy salads, with nuts, dried fruit, and cubes of sweet potato; broil, mix with a little fresh salsa, sprinkle with cheese, and fill whole-wheat tortillas; mix ground turkey with tarragon and chives to create delicious burgers; dice and add to a breakfast frittata instead of bacon.

SEE: TURKEY, PEANUT & MANGO SALAD, P. 83; WILD RICE & TURKEY SALAD, P. 84; GRILLED TURKEY SANDWICH, P. 86; TURKEY BURGERS WITH SWEET POTATO WEDGES, P. 102.

Brazil nuts

✔ Stabilize mood
✔ Balance hormones
✔ Improve energy levels and memory
✔ Prevent anxiety

Brazil nuts are the best natural source of selenium, a mineral with a host of health benefits, many of which relate to stress and its symptoms. They are also rich in healthy fats that can reduce inflammation and the risk of heart disease, as well as the B vitamins that directly affect the health of the nervous system.

They are rich in ...

→ Zinc, which is drained by chronic stress and anxiety, and boosts healthy immunity, libido, hormone balance, energy levels, and memory
→ Selenium, which helps to balance mood and prevent anxiety and depression
→ The B vitamins, reducing the impact of stress on the mind and body
→ Omega oils, easing inflammation and promoting heart health
→ Magnesium, aiding better absorption of energy from food and making sure of healthy nerve function

Use in ... your morning muesli—just a handful gives you the full recommended daily allowance of selenium; dip in dark chocolate for extra stress relief; toss into a salad with romaine lettuce, cubes of feta cheese, and a handful of golden raisins; coarsely chop and add to toppings for crisps or casseroles.

SEE: CRANBERRY & APPLE CRISP, P. 114; DARK CHOCOLATE FONDUE WITH FRUIT & NUTS, P. 122.

Blueberries

✔ Improve energy levels
✔ Reduce blood pressure
✔ Decrease the physical and emotional impact of stress
✔ Reduce inflammation
✔ Enhance concentration and memory

Something of a superstar in the superfood arena, blueberries have a wealth of benefits and high levels of antioxidants, which repair and protect your body from the effects of stress. Blueberries also boost energy levels and balance moods, making it that much easier to deal with the stress in your life.

They are rich in ...
→ Antioxidant nutrients, such as anthocyanins, which lower blood pressure, protect the nervous system and digestive tract, encourage optimum brain function, and balance blood sugar
→ Vitamin C, boosting immunity and reducing the impact of the stress hormone cortisol, affecting both body and mind
→ Fiber, balancing blood sugar levels
→ The B vitamins, helping to boost metabolism and energy levels, and encourage a healthy nervous system

Use in ... your morning cereal; blend in a food processor with plain yogurt and a little honey for a delicious fruit fool; add to pancakes or whole-grain muffins; use frozen blueberries as the basis for smoothies; toss in a salad with a little goat cheese and sliced almonds.

SEE: BLUEBERRY & OAT MUFFINS, P. 40; BLUEBERRY & LEMON ICE CREAM, P. 110; BLUEBERRY WHIP, P. 120.

Pistachios

✔ Reduce the effects of high blood pressure
✔ Balance blood sugar
✔ Encourage heart health
✔ Ease inflammation
✔ Boost energy levels

Pistachios are packed with essential nutrients, with high levels of magnesium and the B vitamins that give your immune system a boost and healthy fats that help protect your heart.

They are rich in ...
→ Vitamins A and E, which can help to prevent inflammation that causes digestive disturbances, aches, and pains
→ Omega oils, reducing inflammation, encouraging brain and heart health, and supporting the immune system
→ Vitamin B_6, which is essential for the supply of oxygenated blood to maintain energy levels and is also required for healthy immunity and nervous system
→ Protein, fiber, and healthy fats, helping to balance blood sugar

Use in ... fruit and vegetable salads for color and crunch; gently roast to enhance the omega-3 content and eat as the perfect snack; add to muesli or sprinkle over cereal or yogurt; stir-fry with chicken, crunchy vegetables, and ginger; crush to make a crust for lamb or beef before roasting.

SEE: APRICOT PUREE WITH YOGURT & PISTACHIOS, P. 39; BAKED BANANAS, P. 112; BLUEBERRY WHIP, P. 120.

Apricots

- ✔ Ease muscle tension and headaches
- ✔ Reduce palpitations
- ✔ Boost the immune system
- ✔ Protect against damage caused by stress
- ✔ Boost energy

Apricots contain high levels of magnesium, the "antistress" mineral that decreases the release of the stress hormone cortisol. They are rich in antioxidants, which help to protect the body from the impact of stress, and contain plenty of iron to help your red blood cells carry fatigue-busting oxygen throughout your body.

They are rich in ...

- → Magnesium, helping to reduce heart palpitations, relax muscles, encourage restful sleep, and support a healthy nervous system
- → Fiber, encouraging healthy digestion and absorption of nutrients from food
- → Beta-carotene and lycopene, antioxidants that encourage heart health and boost immunity
- → Iron, helpful for boosting immunity and energy levels

Use in ... both savory and sweet salads; dried apricots are delicious in chicken dishes for a Middle Eastern flavor; stir into whole-grain pancake batter; blend with a frozen banana and plain yogurt with live cultures for an energy-boosting smoothie; stew with water and a little honey for a delicious breakfast compote.

SEE: APRICOT PUREE WITH YOGURT & PISTACHIOS, P. 39; APRICOT, MANGO & PINEAPPLE SMOOTHIE, P. 62.

Spinach

- ✔ Prevents blood pressure surges
- ✔ Relaxes muscles
- ✔ Encourages restorative sleep
- ✔ Reduces anxiety
- ✔ Regulates stress hormones
- ✔ Promotes well-being

Spinach not only aids relaxation and promotes a feeling of calm, largely due to its high magnesium content, but it is rich in iron to fight fatigue, and helps to mop up excess cortisol levels in the bloodstream. Folic acid and the other B vitamins encourage a healthy nervous system, and even aid concentration and memory.

It's rich in ...

- → Fiber, balancing blood sugar and encouraging healthy digestion
- → Anti-inflammatory chemicals neoxanthin and violaxanthin, which reduce inflammation and pain
- → Peptides, helping to lower blood pressure
- → Vitamin K, good for a healthy nervous system and brain function

Use in ... soups, stews, and casseroles, adding it toward the end of cooking; use instead of lettuce in sandwiches and salads; add to cheese and chives for a light omelet filling; blend with ricotta cheese, garlic, and lightly steamed butternut squash for a delicious pasta sauce or topping for baked potatoes.

SEE: WARM SPINACH SALAD, P. 79; ROOT VEGETABLE STEW WITH POMEGRANATE SALSA, P. 94.

Sweet potatoes

✔ Reduce inflammation
✔ Regulate blood sugar levels
✔ Encourage healthy digestion
✔ Encourage relaxation
✔ Lift mood

A great source of fiber, sweet potatoes can ease digestive complaints and steady blood sugar levels. Their bright color indicates a wealth of antioxidant vitamins, and other key chemicals that can help to reduce the impact of stress on your body and mind, and prevent inflammatory conditions often associated with stress.

They are rich in ...
→ Vitamin B_6, supporting the nervous system, encouraging relaxation, and preventing heart disease
→ Vitamin C, helping to reduce the stress hormone cortisol in the body, boost immunity, and ease digestion
→ Vitamin D, encouraging the health of your heart and nerves, easing fatigue, and balancing moods
→ Magnesium, promoting restful sleep and aid relaxation

Use in ... soups, curries, casseroles, and stews; mash with a little reduced-fat or sour cream or Greek yogurt and black pepper as a delicious side dish; roast sweet potato wedges in olive oil as an alternative to fries; cook in their skins and top with tuna mixed with a little Greek yogurt, the juice of a lime, and a handful of chopped cilantro.

SEE: SWEET POTATO & CABBAGE SOUP, P. 66; ROOT VEGETABLE STEW WITH POMEGRANATE SALSA, P. 94; WILD MUSHROOM STROGANOFF & MASHED SWEET POTATO, P. 98; BAKED SWEET POTATOES WITH VEGETABLE CHILI, P. 100.

Apples

✔ Balance blood sugar
✔ Support the liver
✔ Reduce the stress hormone cortisol
✔ Ease depression
✔ Encourage digestion

The humble apple contains a host of nutrients that work to reduce the production of the damaging stress hormone cortisol, while having an important balancing effect on blood sugar. Rich in antioxidants, apples will support almost every part of your body in times of stress.

They are rich in ...
→ Quercetin, a nutrient that supports the immune system, reduces cortisol production, and encourages healthy brain function
→ Phosphorus and iron, which repair damage caused by stress
→ Pectin, a soluble fiber that aids digestion and promotes the health of the digestive tract, as well as balancing blood sugar
→ Sulfur, which helps support liver function

Use in ... red cabbage dishes for extra flavor; stuff a chicken breast with apples, walnuts, thyme, and whole-grain bread crumbs; mix with honey and raisins, top with an oat and nut crumb toppin, and bake for a satisfying dessert; puree as an accompaniment to pork or mackerel.

SEE: APPLE & YOGURT MUESLI, P. 36; APPLE, PEAR & CHERRY COMPOTE, P. 38; GOAT CHEESE, APPLE & WALNUT SALAD, P. 76; CRANBERRY & APPLE CRISP, P. 114.

Grapes

✔ Reduce the risk of high blood pressure
✔ Ease depression
✔ Encourage heart health
✔ Help prevent stomach ulcers
  and indigestion
✔ Improve memory and concentration

Both green and black grapes—particularly the seeds and skins—contain crucial vitamins, minerals, and other nutrients that can ease the impact of stress on the body, while encouraging healthy digestion and even easing headaches. Grapes are a traditional remedy for fatigue, probably because of their high iron content.

They are rich in ...
→ Manganese and potassium, which lower blood pressure, boost immunity, and help prevent depression
→ Resveratrol, which encourages heart health, lowers sugar and fat levels in the blood, and reduces blood pressure
→ Beneficial bacteria, which encourage digestion and reduce the risk of stomach ulcers
→ Antioxidant nutrients and chemicals that reduce inflammation, protect the heart, and reduce stress-related damage to cells

Use in ... salads with a little feta cheese and toasted almonds; freeze grapes for a sweet, refreshing snack; serve halved with walnuts, cooked chicken, and lettuce in a honey-yogurt dressing; roast grapes alongside pork; add red grapes, scallions, and sliced apricots to boiled rice and stir in a creamy yogurt dressing.

SEE: GOAT CHEESE, APPLE & WALNUT SALAD, P. 76; DARK CHOCOLATE FONDUE WITH FRUIT & NUTS, P. 122.

Cherries

✔ Reduce inflammation and pain
✔ Aid relaxation and encourage sleep
✔ Boost concentration
✔ Ease depression
✔ Reduce cravings
✔ Enhance libido

Both sweet and sour cherries are packed with nutrients that can affect everything from your sense of well-being to your heart health and risk of diabetes. Cherries can ease headaches and tension-related aches and pains, and protect the body against disease and the effects of stress.

They are rich in ...
→ Melatonin, a hormone that helps promote restful sleep and has a calming effect
→ Anthocyanins, plant chemicals that block inflammation and pain (including headaches) that cause or are caused by stress
→ Tyrosine, an amino acid that is required for restful sleep, improved mood, virility, and concentration
→ Fiber, helping to control blood sugar and aid digestion

Use in ... a morning smoothie with yogurt with live cultures; cherry juice—sour cherry juice in particular—will ease digestive problems and headaches quickly; dip in dark chocolate for a delicious, nutritious treat; dried or frozen cherries make a healthy snack; add to whole-grain muffins or pancakes; make a cherry sauce for pork or game dishes.

SEE: CHERRY & CINNAMON PARFAIT, P. 116; SOUR CHERRY CHOCOLATE BROWNIE CAKES, P. 124.

Brown rice

✔ Reduces cortisol levels
✔ Eases anxiety
✔ Balances blood sugar
✔ Eases headaches
✔ Lowers blood pressure
✔ Boosts energy levels

An excellent source of fiber and numerous vitamins and minerals, brown rice also contains plenty of tryptophan, the amino acid that increases serotonin and melatonin levels in the body, encouraging a sense of well-being and restful sleep. It acts like a brush in the digestive tract, and encourages the absorption of nutrients.

It's rich in ...

→ The B vitamins, supporting the nervous system, encouraging even moods, and improving concentration
→ Manganese, good for a healthy nervous system and energy production
→ Selenium, encouraging immunity, balancing moods, and promoting heart health
→ Magnesium, helping to relax the nervous system, reduce blood pressure, lower the incidence of headaches, prevent muscle spasms, and encourage restful sleep

Use in ... a delicious salad with berries, seeds, nuts, scallions, herbs, and a light vinaigrette dressing; make brown rice pudding with soy milk, cinnamon, nutmeg, golden raisins, and honey; stir in sautéed mushrooms and leeks for a delicious side dish; top with grilled chicken, fresh salsa, and grated cheese for a Mexican-style treat.

SEE: MEDITERRANEAN BROWN RICE SALAD, P. 82; BROWN RICE PUDDING, P. 113.

Mushrooms

✔ Balance blood sugar levels
✔ Improve health of the liver and endocrine (hormonal) system
✔ Lift mood
✔ Encourage immunity

A rich source of protective, mood-lifting selenium, mushrooms retain their nutrients no matter how they are cooked. They contain natural insulin, which helps to balance blood sugar levels and restore a sense of calm.

They are rich in ...

→ Polysaccharides, which have been shown to boost the immune system
→ Copper, helping to produce blood cells and maintain heart health
→ Potassium, which lowers blood pressure and reduces the risk of stroke
→ Niacin, encouraging the health of the nervous system

Use in ... stews, soups, stir-fries, and casseroles; sauté in a little olive oil and parsley, and add to omelets or frittatas; slice and toss into a warm spinach salad; pan-fry with garlic and shallots and serve on whole-grain toast.

SEE: SCRAMBLED EGGS ON BROILED MUSHROOMS, P. 46; BACON & MUSHROOM FRITTATA, P. 47; BROILED MUSHROOM & GARLIC WRAPS, P. 69; WARM SPINACH SALAD, P. 79; WILD MUSHROOM STROGANOFF & MASHED SWEET POTATO, P. 98; CHICKEN & BARLEY RISOTTO, P. 105.

Beets

✔ Aphrodisiac
✔ Aids relaxation
✔ Encourages a sense of well-being
✔ Lowers blood pressure
✔ Boosts energy levels
✔ Promotes nervous system health

Beets are an abundant source of dozens of vitamins and minerals, and they are one of the richest sources of energy-boosting iron. They contains betaine and tryptophan to ease depression and lift mood.

They are rich in ...

→ Folate, which helps to build tissue and red blood cells, boosting energy levels
→ Betalains, plant chemicals that have strong anti-inflammatory and antioxidant properties
→ Nitrates, which have been shown to lower stress-related high blood pressure within an hour
→ Boron, which can help to improve virility in both men and women

Use in ... borscht, an Eastern European soup; roast and top with feta cheese and toasted walnuts for a delicious, nutritious salad; juice and serve on crushed ice for a mood-boosting breakfast or snack; roast until tender, puree with a dash of horseradish, and serve with toasted pita bread or crudités.

SEE: ROASTED BEET & FETA SALAD WITH ALMONDS, P. 74; MEDITERRANEAN BROWN RICE SALAD, P. 82; ROOT VEGETABLE STEW WITH POMEGRANATE SALSA, P. 94.

Avocado

✔ Reduces cholesterol
✔ Regulates blood pressure
✔ Boosts immunity
✔ Eases digestion
✔ Balances blood sugar levels
✔ Increases absorption of nutrients from other foods

Avocado contains more than 25 key nutrients, including the B vitamins and potassium, encouraging the health of your nervous system. The healthy fats it contains can help to promote heart health, while regulating blood pressure. It contains high levels of vitamin E, boosting immunity and improving skin health.

It's rich in ...

➔ Beta-sitosterol, lowering unhealthy cholesterol
➔ Potassium, controlling blood pressure
➔ Fibre and monounsaturated fats, balancing blood sugar levels, and preventing insulin resistance, a common side effect of stress
➔ Folic acid, pantothenic acid, and vitamin K, reducing stress levels and improving the health of the nervous system

Use in ... spinach salads, to increase the uptake of nutrients by up to 200 percent; chop with a little fresh chile, diced onion, and tomato for an instant guacamole; puree into smoothies for an energy-boosting snack; stuff with chopped egg and top with chives for an easy, satisfying lunch.

SEE: GUACAMOLE WITH TORTILLA BITES, P. 54; AVOCADO WITH YOGURT DRESSING, P. 57; WARM SPINACH SALAD, P. 79.

Eggs

✔ Promote heart health
✔ Regulate mood
✔ Encourage alertness
✔ Boost health of nerves and brain
✔ Raise energy levels
✔ Support adrenal glands

Very few foods are as rich in key nutrients as eggs, and their high protein levels not only balance blood sugar, but also provide a good source of sustainable energy. Rich in the B vitamins that support the nervous system, eggs are undoubtedly an essential part of any antistress diet.

They are rich in ...

➔ Tryptophan, which helps to regulate mood and encourages sleep
➔ Tyrosine, which promotes mental activity and concentration
➔ Protein, encouraging overall health and helping to stabilize blood sugar and energy levels
➔ Pantothenic acid, the "antistress vitamin" that supports the adrenal glands

Use in ... lightly cooked omelets stuffed with spinach and mushrooms; boiled eggs; poach and serve on smoked salmon and whole-grain toast; braise in chopped tomatoes and chile for a nutritious Mexican breakfast; scramble and wrap in a soft flour tortilla for an easy lunch or breakfast burrito; boil and mash with a little yogurt with live cultures and dill and serve on a bed of lettuce or a slice of whole-grain bread.

SEE: TURKISH POACHED EGGS WITH YOGURT, P. 44; SCRAMBLED EGGS ON BROILED MUSHROOMS, P. 46; BACON & MUSHROOM FRITTATA, P. 47; HERBY SMOKED SALMON OMELET, P. 48; STUFFED EGGS, P. 60.

Cinnamon

✔ Controls blood sugar levels
✔ Boosts immunity
✔ Encourages brain function
✔ Protects against heart disease
✔ Reduces inflammation
✔ Reduces levels of the stress hormone cortisol

Cinnamon has long been used for medicinal purposes, and studies have found that it not only lowers blood sugar levels, but also boosts energy levels and eases the impact of stress. Its smell has been shown to improve brain function and memory.

It's rich in ...

→ MCHP, a chemical that reduces blood sugar levels and some forms of anxiety
→ Anti-inflammatory chemicals, which promote heart health, protect arteries from stress-related damage, and reduce muscle and joint pain
→ Calcium, easing anxiety and restoring nervous system function
→ Essential oils that boost immunity and encourage healthy digestion

Use in ... oatmeal; stir into warm, freshly pressed apple juice; use to flavor unsweetened fruit purees and serve with yogurt with live cultures; add a teaspoon to chicken and lamb casseroles for warmth and flavor; steep cinnamon sticks in boiling water to make a nutritious, stimulating tea; sprinkle over mashed bananas and serve on whole-wheat toast.

SEE: EDAMAME HUMMUS, P. 58; ROOT VEGETABLE STEW WITH POMEGRANATE SALSA, P. 94; MANGO BRÛLÉE, P. 108; BROWN RICE PUDDING, P. 113; CRANBERRY & APPLE CRISP, P. 114; CHERRY & CINNAMON PARFAIT, P. 116.

Cranberries

✔ Balance blood sugar levels
✔ Encourage heart health
✔ Reduce inflammation
✔ Protect the brain from stress-related damage
✔ Boost immunity
✔ Encourage healthy digestion

Cranberries are one of the richest sources of vitamin C and other antioxidant nutrients, which play an important role in reducing the damaging effects of stress, while encouraging overall health and well-being. Full of fiber, they help regulate digestion and blood sugar levels.

They are rich in ...

→ Phytonutrients, which reduce inflammation, ease muscle and joint pain, and improve oral health, digestion, and heart health
→ Proanthocyanidins, proven to boost immunity
→ Resveratrol, piceatanno,l and pterostilbene, which can help to prevent heart and circulatory damage caused by stress
→ Chemicals that can help to prevent stomach ulcers

Use in ... chicken or lamb stews or stews; add dried cranberries to your breakfast cereal or muesli; mix with apples and cinnamon and top with oats for a tasty crisp; juice, sweeten with a little maple syrup, and gently heat for a nourishing warm drink; toss dried cranberries into a salad with dark green leaves and goat cheese; fill the core of an apple with cranberries and a little brown sugar and cinnamon and bake for a tangy, healthy dessert.

SEE: CRANBERRY & APPLE CRISP, P. 114.

Yogurt with live active cultures

- ✔ Encourages healthy digestion
- ✔ Reduces risk of high blood pressure
- ✔ Increases the absorption of the stress-relieving B vitamins
- ✔ Boosts immunity
- ✔ Enables restful sleep
- ✔ Eases anxiety

....

Yogurt rich in probiotics (healthy bacteria) is often tolerated by people who are intolerant to lactose. It is a great source of calcium and the B vitamins. By encouraging the health of the digestive tract, yogurt can improve digestion, immunity, and emotional health by promoting communication between the digestive tract and the brain.

....

It's rich in ...

- → Friendly bacteria, which encourage the health of the digestive tract, help it absorb nutrients more efficiently, and enhance immune function
- → Probiotics, which have been shown to impact the brain chemistry involved in stress, anxiety, and depression
- → Calcium, which acts on the nervous system and encourages restful sleep
- → The B vitamins, for a healthy nervous system and improved relaxation

....

Use in ... fruit smoothies; mix with chives, sea salt, and black pepper to top baked potatoes; use instead of milk on cereal and muesli; blend with herbs, spice,s and a little olive oil for a creamy dip; add lemon juice, lemon zest, and dill to make a satisfying salad dressing; stir into soups and curries instead of cream or coconut milk.

....

SEE: APPLE AND YOGURT MUESLI, P. 36; TURKISH POACHED EGGS WITH YOGURT, P. 44; RASPBERRY YOGURT GRATIN, P. 121.

Popcorn

- ✔ Encourages healthy digestion
- ✔ Balances blood sugar
- ✔ Protects against stress-related diseases
- ✔ Boosts energy levels

....

Amazingly, popcorn contains more antioxidants than fruit and vegetables and, as a whole grain, it is an excellent source of the B vitamins, fiber, slow-release carbohydrates, and good-quality protein. Watch the salt and the butter, which can add unnecessary calories.

....

It's rich in ...

- → Polyphenols, antioxidant plant chemicals that can protect the body from disease and stress-related damage
- → Ferulic acid, which protects against cancer, diabetes, cardiovascular problems, and diseases of the nervous system
- → Fiber, aiding healthy digestion and enhanced absorption of nutrients from food
- → The B vitamins, improving nerve function and helping the body produce energy efficiently

....

Use in ... salads and soups instead of croutons; mist with olive oil and season with a little sea salt and a lot of black pepper as a snack; flavor with finely chopped fresh herbs, such as dill, cilantro, and parsley; for a sweet treat, drizzle with a little maple syrup and throw in a handful of chopped almonds; sprinkle with ground cinnamon or ginger for added zing; crush and use as a coating for chicken or fish in place of bread crumbs or flour.

....

Almonds

✔ Stabilize blood sugar levels
✔ Lower bad cholesterol
✔ Boost energy levels
✔ Promote relaxation
✔ Protect your heart

Almonds contain more nutrients than any other nut and are an excellent source of vitamin E, calcium, magnesium, phosphorus, and iron, all of which play a role in coping with the stresses of day-to-day life and encourage a sense of calm. The healthy fats they contain help to prevent heart disease and decrease inflammation in the body.

They are rich in ...

→ Vitamin E, an antioxidant that has been shown to prevent damage caused by stress, while boosting immunity
→ The B vitamins and magnesium, which help produce serotonin, regulating mood and relieving the symptoms of stress
→ Zinc, which fights the negative effects of stress
→ Calcium, promoting restful sleep and encouraging relaxation

Use in ... salads with cheese and dried fruit; spread almond butter on toast; use almond milk on cereal or in hot drinks; add to muesli or crisp toppings; coat chicken breasts or fish with ground almonds; make almond pesto, using almonds in place of pine nuts.

SEE: ROASTED BEET & FETA SALAD WITH ALMONDS, P. 74; BAKED BANANAS, P. 112; CRANBERRY & APPLE CRISP, P. 114; RICOTTA, PLUM & ALMOND CAKE, P. 118; DARK CHOCOLATE FONDUE WITH FRUIT & NUTS, P. 122.

Bananas

✔ Protect the nervous system
✔ Encourage heart health
✔ Lift mood
✔ Promote a sense of calm
✔ Boost energy

Bananas are effectively little packages of energy, with a host of key nutrients to help your body work at optimum level. Most important, they provide plenty of potassium (often deficient in the Western diet), which is required for a healthy nervous system and balanced moods.

They are rich in ...

→ Potassium, which improves the health of your heart and nervous system; potassium also helps to lower blood pressure
→ Tryptophan, helping the body produce serotonin, which has a calming effect on the brain
→ Vitamin B_6, encouraging the production of oxygen-carrying red blood cells and disease-fighting antibodies
→ Fiber, improving digestion and balance blood sugar levels

Use in ... fruit smoothies; fruit salads; mashed on whole-grain toast with a sprinkling of cinnamon; baked with a dash of vanilla and some maple syrup, served with yogurt with live cultures; broil and serve alongside duck or teriyaki pork chops.

SEE: BAKED BANANAS, P. 112.

WHAT'S YOUR PROBLEM?

Relieve symptoms of stress by eating the foods that target them. Decide which symptoms affect you and choose from the foods and recipes that can relieve them. There is an icon by each symptom. These icons are used throughout the recipe section to highlight which recipes can help combat which symptoms.

Headaches

Whole grains, salmon, olive oil, ginger, nuts, seeds, berries, cucumber, melon, tomatoes, grapefruit, apricots, papaya, peaches, cinnamon, rosemary, oats

Recipes Include:
Apricot puree with yogurt & pistachios, p. 39; Salmon with mashed beans & celeriac, p. 90; Gingery chickpea curry, p. 96; Cranberry & apple crisp, p. 114.

Muscle tension/ pain

Ginger, salmon, sour cherries, yogurt, eggs, peanuts, turkey, lentils, almonds

Recipes Include:
Apple, pear & cherry compote, p. 38; Turkish poached eggs with yogurt, p. 44; Green lentils with flaked salmon, p. 72; Root vegetable stew with pomegranate salsa, p. 94; Sour cherry chocolate brownie cakes, p. 124.

Digestive problems (diarrhea/ stomachache/ indigestion/ constipation)

Salmon, ginger, bananas, rye bread, cinnamon, apples, spinach, edamame (soybeans), sweet potatoes, yogurt, berries, avocado, barley, flaxseed, brown rice

Recipes Include:
Apple & yogurt muesli, p. 36; Tzatziki with rye toast, p. 52; Warm spinach salad, p. 79; Mediterranean brown rice salad, p. 82.

Dizziness

Poultry, beans, eggs, tofu, yogurt, fish, whole grains, bananas, peaches, apricots, spinach, asparagus, peas

Recipes Include:
Salmon & asparagus roll ups, p. 50; Turkey burgers with sweet potato wedges, p. 102; Chicken & barley risotto, p. 105; Baked bananas, p. 112.

Breathlessness

Nuts, seeds, beans, dried apricots, raisins, golden raisins, spinach, lean red meat, broccoli
Recipes Include: Apricot, mango & pineapple smoothie, p. 62; Goat cheese, apple & walnut salad, p. 76; Lamb & bean stew, p. 106; Dark chocolate fondue with fruit & nuts, p. 122.

High blood pressure

Skim milk, spinach, sunflower seeds, beans, baked potatoes, bananas, edamame (soybeans), salmon, dark chocolate
Recipes Include: Edamame hummus, p. 58; Chocolate & almond squares, p. 63; Gingered tofu & mango salad, p. 80; Potato & onion tortilla, p. 97.

Irritability

Tuna, salmon, mackerel, oats, black beans, pumpkin seeds, artichokes, dark chocolate, spinach, bananas, peanuts, brown rice, cashews
Recipes Include: Fruity mango oat bars, p. 64; Smoked mackerel pasta salad, p. 73; Turkey, peanut & mango salad, p. 83; Wild mushroom stroganoff & mashed sweet potato, p. 98.

Poor concentration & forgetfulness

Broccoli, Brussels sprouts, cauliflower, spinach, berries, cherries, eggplants, onions, red apples, beets, leeks, apricots, grapes, lentils, edamame (soybeans), oranges, fish, dark chocolate, whole grains
Recipes Include: Edamame hummus, p. 58; Roasted beet & feta salad with almonds, p. 74.

Anxiety

Brazil nuts, peaches, blueberries, acacia berries, almonds, dark chocolate, oats, brown rice, edamame (soybeans), bananas, peanuts, avocado, melon, lettuce, raspberries, fava beans

Recipes Include:
Apple & yogurt muesli, p. 36; Guacamole with tortilla bites, p. 54; Chocolate & almond squares, p. 63; Warm spinach salad, p. 79; Blueberry whip, p. 120.

Mood swings

Whole grains, beans, tuna, salmon, halibut, cheese, yogurt, green tea, dark chocolate, mushrooms, almonds, brazil nuts, pistachios, blueberries, pomegranate, cinnamon, leafy green vegetables

Recipes Include:
Herbed smoked salmon omelet, p. 48; Broiled mushroom & garlic wraps, p. 69; Wild mushroom stroganoff & mashed sweet potatoes, p. 98.

Depression/ unhappiness

Salmon, whole grains, oats, nuts, seeds, beans, brown rice, brewer's yeast (or Marmite), quinoa, cabbage, brazil nuts, dark chocolate, sweet potatoes, kiwifruit, bell peppers, oranges, carrots, melon, apricots

Recipes Include:
Garlic & bean pâté, p. 56; Bacon & cannellini bean soup, p. 68; Root vegetable stew with pomegranate salsa, p. 94.

Chest pains/ palpitations

Whole grains, nuts, seeds, salmon, mackerel, fresh fruit and vegetables

Recipes Include:
Apricot, mango & pineapple smoothie, p. 62; Smoked mackerel pasta salad, p. 73; Baked sweet potatoes with vegetable chili, p. 100; Herbed quinoa with lemon & chicken, p. 104.

Frequent colds & infections

Garlic, potatoes, horseradish, strawberries (and other berries), ginger, yogurt, oats, apricots, asparagus, mangoes, cauliflower, mushrooms, sweet potatoes, shellfish, brazil nuts, peaches, broccoli, sunflower seeds, celery

Recipes Include:
Spicy shrimp kebabs with wild rice, p. 91; Gingery chickpea curry, p. 96; Mango brûlée, p. 108.

Loss of libido/desire

Celery, shellfish, pineapple, bananas, avocado, almonds, mangoes, peaches, strawberries, eggs, figs, garlic, dark chocolate

Recipes Include:
Stuffed eggs, p. 60; Apricot, mango & pineapple smoothie, p. 62; Lemony scallop skewers with arugula, p. 70; Thai mussel curry with ginger, p. 92.

Sleep problems

Popcorn, oats, dairy produce, peanuts, grapes, edamame (soybeans), seeds, beans, eggs, honey, almonds, avocado, bananas, seafood, turkey, papaya, mushrooms, brown rice

Recipes Include:
Blueberry & oat muffins, p. 40; Edamame hummus, p. 58; Gingered tofu & mango salad, p. 80; Turkey burgers with sweet potato wedges, p. 102.

Low energy

Dried cranberries, pistachios, blueberries, oranges, spinach, salmon, mackerel, almonds, olive oil, green tea, oatmeal, beans, cinnamon, ginger, garlic, turmeric, brown rice, broccoli, sesame seeds, avocado

Recipes Include:
Green lentil salad with flaked salmon, p. 72; Root vegetable stew with pomegranate salsa, p. 94; Cranberry & apple crisp, p. 114.

PUTTING IT ALL TOGETHER

Meal Planner	Monday	Tuesday	Wednesday
Breakfast	Breakfast cereal bars, p. 43	Apple & yogurt muesli, p. 36	Blueberry & oat muffins, p. 40
Morning snack	Tzatziki with rye toast, p. 52	Edamame hummus, p. 58	Salmon & asparagus roll ups, p. 50
Lunch	Sweet potato & cabbage soup, p. 66	Wild rice & turkey salad, p. 84	Bacon & cannellini bean soup, p. 68
Afternoon snack	Avocado with yogurt dressing, p. 57	Stuffed eggs, p. 60	Fruity mango oat bars, p. 64
Dinner	Salmon with mashed beans & celeriac, p. 90	Lamb & bean stew, p. 106	Wild mushroom stroganoff & mashed sweet potatoes, p98
Dessert	Ricotta, plum & almond cake, p. 118	Mango brûlée, p. 108	Raspberry yogurt gratin, p. 121

WEEK 1

Thursday

Apricot puree with yogurt & pistachios, p. 39

Chocolate & almond squares, p. 63

Goat cheese, apple & walnut salad, p. 76

Popcorn

Root vegetable stew with pomegranate salsa, p. 94

Brown rice pudding, p. 113

Friday

Scrambled eggs on broiled mushrooms, p. 46

Broccoli florets & carrot sticks with Tzatziki, p. 52

Lemony scallop skewers with arugula, p. 70

Black olive tapenade with rice cakes, p. 53

Thai mussel curry with ginger, p. 92

Sour cherry chocolate brownie cakes, p. 124

Saturday

Bacon & mushroom frittata, p. 47

Apricot, mango & pineapple smoothie, p. 62

Gingered tofu & mango salad, p. 80

Dark chocolate covered brazil nuts

Potato & onion tortilla, p. 97

Baked bananas, p. 112

Sunday

Herbed smoked salmon omelet, p. 48

Guacamole with tortilla bites, p. 54

Warm spinach salad, p. 79

A chunk of cheese and a bunch of grapes

Herbed quinoa with lemon & chicken, p. 104

Cranberry & apple crisp, p. 114

Meal Planner	Monday	Tuesday	Wednesday
Breakfast	Apple, pear & cherry compote, p. 38	Quinoa porridge with pomegranate, p. 42	Scrambled eggs on broiled mushrooms, p. 46
Morning snack	Garlic & bean pâté, p. 56	Salmon & asparagus roll ups, p. 50	Black olive tapenade with rice cakes, p. 53
Lunch	Watermelon & feta salad, p. 78	Broiled mushroom & garlic wraps, p. 69	Turkey, peanut & mango salad, p. 83
Afternoon snack	Stuffed eggs, p. 60	Popcorn sprinkled with cinnamon	Dark chocolate covered brazil nuts
Dinner	Fish & mango curry with brown rice, p. 88	Spicy shrimp kebabs with wild rice, p. 91	Gingery chickpea curry, p. 96
Dessert	Blueberry & lemon ice cream, p. 110	Dark chocolate fondue with fruit & nuts, p. 122	Blueberry whip, p. 120

WEEK 2

Thursday

Blueberry & oat muffins, p. 40

Apricot, mango & pineapple smoothie, p. 62

Green lentils with flaked salmon, p. 72

Chocolate & almond squares, p. 63

Chicken & barley risotto, p. 105

Cherry & cinnamon parfait, p. 116

Friday

Apple & yogurt muesli, p. 36

Avocado with yogurt dressing, p. 57

Grilled Turkey Sandwich, p. 86

Banana

Baked sweet potatoes with vegetable chili, p. 100

Brown rice pudding, p. 113

Saturday

Herbed smoked salmon omelet, p. 48

Edamame hummus with rice cakes, p. 58

Roasted beet & feta salad with almonds, p. 74

Garlic & bean pâté, p. 56

Thai mussel curry with ginger, p. 92

Ricotta, plum & almond cake, p. 118

Sunday

Turkish poached eggs with yogurt, p. 44

Guacamole with tortilla bites, p. 54

Mediterranean brown rice salad, p. 82

Fruity mango oat bars, p. 64

Turkey burgers with sweet potato wedges, p. 102

Sour cherry chocolate brownie cakes, p. 124

CALM
RECIPES

APPLE & YOGURT MUESLI

A filling breakfast to balance blood sugar and provide slow-release energy through the morning.

Preparation time: 15 minutes, plus soaking
Cooking time: 10 minutes
Serves 4
....

2 cups **rolled oats**
¼ cup **wheat germ**
¼ cup **rye flakes**
⅔ cup **millet flakes**
½ cup coarsely chopped **hazelnuts**
½ cup coarsely chopped **almonds**
⅓ cup **golden raisins**
⅓ cup coarsely chopped **dried apricots**
⅓ cup coarsely chopped **dried dates**
2 **sweet, crisp apples**, peeled
    and coarsely grated
1¾ cups **apple juice**
2 teaspoons **ground cinnamon**
1 cup **fat-free Greek yogurt**
    with honey
2 teaspoons **flaxseed**
honey, to serve (optional)

Put the rolled oats into a large bowl and stir in the wheat germ, rye flakes, millet flakes, nuts, and dried fruits. Arrange the mixture on a baking sheet and place in a preheated oven, at 325°F, for 10 minutes then let cool.

....

Return the muesli to the mixing bowl and stir in the apples. Add the apple juice and cinnamon and stir well to combine. Let soak for 5–6 minutes.

....

Divide the soaked muesli among 4 serving bowls and spoon the yogurt on top. Sprinkle with the flaxseed and drizzle with a little honey, if desired.

....

APPLE, PEAR & CHERRY COMPOTE

This not only makes a healthy breakfast rich in antioxidants and fiber, but it's great served warm as a dessert.

Preparation time: 20 minutes
Cooking time: 20–25 minutes
Serves 6

4 **sweet, crisp apples**, peeled, cored, and diced
2 **Granny Smith apples**, peeled, cored, and diced
4 **pears**, peeled, cored, and diced
3 tablespoons packed **light brown sugar**
2 tablespoons **water**
½ teaspoon **vanilla extract**
1 cup **dried sour cherries**
plain yogurt with live cultures, to serve

Place the apples, pears, and sugar in a nonstick saucepan with the measured water and bring to a boil. Reduce the heat, cover the pan, and simmer gently for 15–20 minutes, or until the apples are soft and beginning to break down.

Stir in the vanilla and cherries, add a little more water, if necessary, then cover and cook for another 5 minutes. Taste and add a little more sugar, if required.

Transfer to a blender or food processor and blend to create a chunky compote. Serve warm or cold with the yogurt. The compote can be stored in an airtight container in the refrigerator for up to a week.

APRICOT PUREE WITH YOGURT & PISTACHIOS

This fruity puree is bursting with stress-busting magnesium. Serve with yogurt with live active cultures to aid the digestion.

Preparation time: 5 minutes
Cooking time: 25–30 minutes
Serves 6

3 cups **dried apricots**
1⅓ cups **orange juice**
finely grated zest of ½ **orange**

To serve
½ cup **plain yogurt with live cultures** per person
3 tablespoons **raw pistachio nuts**, chopped, per person

Place the apricots, orange juice and orange zest in a nonstick saucepan over medium heat and bring to a boil. Reduce the heat and simmer for 20–25 minutes, or until apricots are plump and juicy.

Remove from the heat, let cool slightly, then transfer to a blender or food processor and blend until smooth. Serve warm or cold, layered with yogurt and chopped pistachios.

The purée can be stored in an airtight container in the refrigerator for up to a week.

BLUEBERRY & OAT MUFFINS

These moist muffins are ideal for breakfast or a midmorning snack—they'll keep you going for hours.

Preparation time: 15 minutes
Cooking time: 20–25 minutes
Makes 12

1 cup **whole-wheat flour**
1⅓ cups **rolled oats**
3 teaspoons **baking powder**
pinch of **salt**
1 teaspoon **ground cinnamon**,
   plus extra for dusting
½ cup firmly packed **light brown sugar**
finely grated zest of ½ **lemon**
finely grated zest of ½ **orange**
1 extra-large **egg**
½ cup **plain yogurt with live active cultures**
½ cup **whole milk** or **lactose-free milk**
4 tablespoons **unsalted butter**, melted
1⅓ cups fresh or frozen **blueberries**

Put the flour, oats, baking powder, salt, cinnamon, sugar, orange zest, and lemon zest into a large bowl and stir until well combined. In a separate bowl, beat together the egg, yogurt, milk, and melted butter and fold gently and quickly into the dry ingredients, mixing until only just combined.

Gently stir the blueberries into the muffin batter and spoon into a 12-section muffin pan lined with paper liners. Dust each muffin with a little extra cinnamon.

Place in a preheated oven, at 400°F, for 20–25 minutes, or until golden and risen. Remove from the pan and cool on a wire rack. Store in an airtight container for up to 4 days.

QUINOA PORRIDGE WITH POMEGRANATE

Quinoa, rich in key amino acids and other nutrients, makes a nutritious, filling and mood-lifting breakfast.

Preparation time: 10 minutes
Cooking time: 25 minutes
Serves 4
....

1¾ cups **quinoa**
2½ cups **skim milk** or **lactose-free milk**,
    plus extra to serve
¼ cup unsweetened **pomegranate juice**
1 teaspoon **honey**
seeds from 1 **pomegranate**

Put the quinoa and milk into a large nonstick saucepan over medium heat and bring to a boil. Reduce the heat to a slow simmer and cook for 20 minutes, or until the milk has been absorbed and the quinoa seeds are plump. Stir frequently and add a little more milk or water if it becomes too dry.

....

Meanwhile, mix the pomegranate juice and honey in a small bowl and add the pomegranate seeds.

....

Divide the porridge among 4 serving bowls, top with the pomegranate mixture, and serve with a little extra milk.

....

BREAKFAST CEREAL BARS

Packed with seeds, nuts, and whole grains, these nutritious bars are perfect for breakfast on the run.

Preparation time: 10 minutes, plus cooling
Cooking time: 35 minutes
Makes 16

6 tablespoons **butter**, softened
2 tablespoons packed **light brown sugar**
2 tablespoons **light corn syrup**
3 cups **millet flakes**
⅓ cup **quinoa**
⅓ cup **dried cherries** or **cranberries**
½ cup **golden raisins**
3 tablespoons **sunflower seeds**
3 tablespoons **sesame seeds**
2½ tablespoons **flaxseed**
½ cup unsweetened **dried coconut**
2 **eggs**, lightly beaten

Beat the butter, sugar, and corn syrup in a mixing bowl with a wooden spoon until pale and creamy. Add all the remaining ingredients and beat well until combined.

Transfer to a greased 11 x 8 inch baking pan and level the surface with the back of a spoon. Place in a preheated oven, at 350°F, for 35 minutes, until deep golden. Let cool in the pan.

Turn out on to a wooden board and carefully cut into 16 bars, using a serrated knife. Store in an airtight container for up to a week.

TURKISH POACHED EGGS WITH YOGURT

Ideal for a lazy weekend breakfast, these delicious poached eggs can also be served with salad for a light lunch.

Preparation time: 10 minutes
Cooking time: 10 minutes
Serves 4
....

4 extra-large **eggs**
3 tablespoons **vinegar**
1 cup **plain yogurt with live active cultures**
1 garlic **clove**, crushed
2 teaspoons **paprika**
1 tablespoon **butter**, melted
1 tablespoon finely chopped dried or fresh **mint**
sea salt and **black pepper**

Bring a saucepan of water to a boil, add the vinegar, and reduce the heat to a slow simmer. One by one, crack the eggs into the water and cook for 3–4 minutes, or until the whites are firm but the yolks still runny.

....

Meanwhile, mix the yogurt and garlic and season to taste. Divide the yogurt among 4 serving plates, and spread into a circle. In a separate small bowl, mix together the paprika and butter.

....

Remove the eggs from the pan with a slotted spoon and arrange on top of the yogurt on the plates. Drizzle with the paprika butter and sprinkle with mint. Serve immediately.

....

SCRAMBLED EGGS ON BROILED MUSHROOMS

Creamy scrambled eggs, served on portabello mushrooms, lift the mood and provide a filling start to the day.

Preparation time: 15 minutes
Cooking time: 10 minutes
Serves 4

4 large **portabello mushrooms**, stems removed
1 teaspoon **olive oil**
½ teaspoon **dried thyme**
6 **eggs**, beaten
2 tablespoons **plain yogurt with live active cultures**
1 teaspoon chopped **chives**
1 teaspoon chopped **dill**
sea salt and **black pepper**

Drizzle the mushrooms with the olive oil, sprinkle with the thyme, and season to taste. Cook under a preheated hot broiler for 8 minutes, until tender, turning once.

Meanwhile, put the eggs, yogurt, chives, and dill into a mixing bowl, season to taste, and beat until smooth. Heat a nonstick saucepan over medium heat and add the egg mixture. Stir constantly until the eggs are smooth, creamy, and just beginning to set.

Transfer the mushrooms to serving plates and top with the scrambled eggs. Season with black pepper and serve immediately.

BACON & MUSHROOM FRITTATA

This is a healthy version of a fried breakfast, with a good boost of the B vitamins to support the nervous system.

Preparation time: 10 minutes, plus cooling
Cooking time: 25–30 minutes
Serves 4

8 large **cremini mushrooms**
1 garlic **clove**, finely chopped (optional)
olive oil spray
4 lean **smoked bacon strips**
6 extra-large **eggs**
1 tablespoon chopped **chives**,
    plus extra to garnish
1 tablespoon **whole-grain mustard**
pat of **butter**
4 large slices of **whole-grain bread**, toasted
sea salt and **black pepper**

Place the mushrooms on an aluminum foil-lined baking sheet and sprinkle with the garlic, if using. Spray with a little olive oil, season to taste, and place in a preheated oven, at 350°F, for 18–20 minutes or until tender. Let until cool enough to handle.

Meanwhile, lay the bacon strips on a foil-lined broiler pan and cook under a preheated medium-hot broiler for 5–6 minutes, turning once, or until slightly crispy. Let until cool enough to handle, then slice thickly.

Place the eggs, chives, and mustard in a bowl, beat together lightly, and season to taste. Heat a large nonstick ovenproof skillet over medium heat, add the butter, and heat until beginning to froth. Pour in the egg mixture and cook for 1–2 minutes, then add the bacon and whole mushrooms, stem sides up. Cook for another 2–3 minutes or until almost set.

Place the pan under a preheated hot broiler and cook for another 2–3 minutes, until set. Cut the frittata into wedges and serve on the toast, garnished with chives.

HERBED SMOKED SALMON OMELET

The omega oils in salmon are good for the heart and brain, so choose this breakfast when you need to run on all cylinders.

Preparation time: 10 minutes
Cooking time: 15 minutes
Serves 4

....

8 extra-large **eggs**
2 **scallions**, thinly sliced
2 tablespoons chopped **chives**
2 tablespoons chopped **chervil**
4 tablespoons **butter**
4 oz **smoked salmon**,
    cut into thin strips
black pepper
baby greens and herb salad, to serve

Put the eggs, scallions, and herbs into a bowl, beat together lightly, and season with black pepper.

....

Heat a skillet over medium-low heat, add one-quarter of the butter, and melt until beginning to froth. Pour in one-quarter of the egg mixture and swirl to cover the bottom of the skillet. Stir gently for 2–3 minutes or until almost set.

....

Sprinkle with one-quarter of the smoked salmon and cook for another 30 seconds or until just set. Fold the omelet in half and slide onto a warm serving plate.

....

Repeat with the remaining ingredients to make 3 more omelets and serve immediately with a baby greens and herb salad.

....

SALMON & ASPARAGUS ROLL UPS

Prepare a few of these tasty little snacks in advance and wrap individually for an instant energy boost.

Preparation time: 10 minutes
Cooking time: 5 minutes
Serves 4

4 large or 8 medium **asparagus spears**
4 slices of **smoked salmon**
2 teaspoons **reduced-fat cream cheese**
1 teaspoon chopped **dill**
finely grated zest of ½ **lemon**
black pepper

Break the woody ends off the asparagus spears, then cook in a saucepan of lightly salted boiling water for about 4 minutes, until just tender. Drain and plunge into a bowl of cold water to refresh.

Meanwhile, mix together the cream cheese, dill, lemon zest, and black pepper and spread the mixture on the smoked salmon slices. When the asparagus is cool, place one large spear or two medium spears at the end of each smoked salmon slice and roll up tightly. Season with more black pepper.

TZATZIKI WITH RYE TOAST

Tzatziki is a nutritious, low-fat dip that can be served with fresh crudités or, in this case, crunchy rye toast.

Preparation time: 15 minutes, plus standing
Cooking time: 5 minutes
Serves 4

....

3 **garlic cloves**, crushed
1½ cups finely chopped **dill**
1½ cups finely chopped **mint**
2 cups finely chopped fresh **cilantro**
½ **cucumber**, seeded and finely chopped
1 small **red chile** seeded and finely chopped
2½ cups **Greek yogurt with live active cultures**
sea salt and **black pepper**
rye bread, to serve

Place all the ingredients in a blender or food processor and blend until smooth. Season to taste, then set aside for at least 1 hour before serving to let the flavors mingle.

....

Thinly slice the rye bread and toast until crisp and lightly browned. Serve with the tzatziki on top. The tzatziki can be kept in an airtight container in the refrigerator for up to 4 days. Stir well before serving.

....

BLACK OLIVE TAPENADE WITH RICE CAKES

Olives prevent cholesterol buildup in the arteries, and anchovies provide brain-nourishing omega-3 oils.

Preparation time: 5 minutes
Serves 4

3 teaspoons **capers**, rinsed and drained
4 canned **anchovy fillets**
1 **garlic clove**, crushed
finely grated zest and juice of 1 **lemon**
2½ cups pitted **black ripe olives**
2 teaspoons chopped **parsley**
3–4 teaspoons **olive oil**
sea salt and **black pepper**
rice cakes or toasted **whole-grain pita breads**, to serve

Place the capers, anchovy fillets, garlic, lemon zest, and lemon juice in a blender or food processor and blend for about 10 seconds, until you have a rough puree.

Add the olives, parsley, and enough olive oil to make a paste. Blend agai,n then season to taste. Serve with rice cakes or toasted whole-grain pita breads.

GUACAMOLE WITH TORTILLA BITES

This is an easy snack or side dish for a Mexican-style feast. The avocados are not just filling, but immensely nutritious.

Preparation time: 10 minutes
Cooking time: 15 minutes
Serves 4

....

4 whole-grain soft flour **tortillas**
1 teaspoon **olive oil**
1 teaspoon **paprika**
3 large, ripe **avocados**, peeled and pitted
3 **scallions**, finely chopped
1 large ripe **tomato**, finely chopped
2 cups fresh finely chopped **cilantro**
finely grated zest and juice of 1 **lime**
2 **garlic cloves**, crushed

Brush the tortillas on both sides with the olive oil and cut into triangles, roughly the shape of store-bought tortilla chips. Transfer to a baking sheet, sprinkle with paprika, and place in a preheated oven, at 400°F, for 10 minutes, until crisp.

Meanwhile, put the avocado into a bowl and mash with the onions, tomato, cilantro, lime zest, lime juice, and garlic until smooth. Serve with the tortilla bites.

Any leftover guacamole can be stored in an airtight container in the refrigerator with the pit of the avocado, which helps to prevent it from browning, for up to 2 days.

GARLIC & BEAN PÂTÉ

Immune-boosting, blood-cleansing garlic accompanies rich pesto and energy-sustaining beans in this tasty dip.

Preparation time: 10 minutes
Serves 4

1 (15 oz) can **great Northern beans**, rinsed and drained
½ cup **cream cheese**
2 **garlic cloves**, chopped
3 teaspoons store-bought **pesto**
2 **scallions**, chopped
1 teaspoon **olive oil**
sea salt and **black pepper**

To serve
cucumber sticks
4 **whole-wheat pita breads**

Place the beans, cream cheese, garlic, and 2 teaspoons of the pesto in a blender or food processor and blend until smooth. Add the scallions, season to taste and blend for another 10 seconds. Spoon into a dish and chill until required.

Mix the remaining pesto with the olive oil and drizzle it over the pâté before serving with cucumber sticks and strips of lightly toasted pita bread.

Any leftover pâté can be stored in an airtight container in the refrigerator for up to 4 days.

AVOCADO WITH YOGURT DRESSING

Avocados, bursting with beneficial fats, are served here with a yogurt dressing as a quick snack or side dish.

Preparation time: 15 minutes
Serves 4

....

2 ripe **avocados**, peeled, pitted, and sliced
1 teaspoon **lemon juice**

Dressing
½ cup **low-fat plain yogurt with
  live active cultures**
4 teaspoons chopped fresh **cilantro**
1 teaspoon chopped **mint**
½ small **red onion**, finely chopped
1 **garlic clove**, finely chopped
1 teaspoon **lemon juice**
finely grated zest of ½ **lemon**

Toss the avocado slices with the lemon juice and arrange on serving plates. Place all the dressing ingredients in a blender or food processor and blend until smooth. Drizzle the dressing over the avocado and serve immediately.

....

Any leftover dressing can be stored in an airtight container in the refrigerator for up to 2 days.

....

EDAMAME HUMMUS

Edamame (soybeans) balance hormones and are a good source of protein. Serve this hummus with whole-wheat toast or pita breads, crudités, or seedy breadsticks.

Preparation time: 10 minutes
Cooking time: 4 minutes
Serves 4
....

1⅔ cups frozen **edamame (soybeans)**
¼ cup **tahini**
½ teaspoon finely grated **lemon** zest
4 teaspoons **lemon juice**
1 **garlic clove**, crushed
1 **scallion**, finely chopped
¾ teaspoon **sea salt**
½ teaspoon **ground cumin**
½ teaspoon **ground coriander**
pinch of **ground cinnamon**
1 tablespoon **olive oil**
2 teaspoons chopped fresh **cilantro**

Cook the beans in a saucepan of lightly salted boiling water for 3–4 minutes, until just tender. Drain and place in a blender or food processor with the tahini, lemon zest, lemon juice, garlic, scallion, salt, and spices and blend until smooth.
....

With the motor still running, slowly pour in the olive oil until the hummus has emulsified. Transfer to a serving dish and sprinkle with the chopped cilantro.
....

Any leftover hummus can be stored in an airtight container in the refrigerator for up to 4 days.
....

STUFFED EGGS

These herbed eggs will appeal to the whole family and provide calming nutrients at the same time.

Preparation time: 15 minutes
Serves 4
....

4 hard-boiled **eggs**, shelled
2 teaspoons **plain yogurt with live active cultures**
1 teaspoon finely chopped **chives**
1 teaspoon finely chopped **dill**
½ teaspoon finely chopped **tarragon**
1 teaspoon finely grated **lemon** zest
sea salt and **black pepper**

Cut the eggs in half lengthwise and remove the yolks. Place the yolks in a small bowl with the remaining ingredients, season to taste, and mash to combine.
....

Arrange the whites, cut sides up, on a serving plate. Carefully spoon the yolk mixture back into the hollows and serve immediately.
....

APRICOT, MANGO & PINEAPPLE SMOOTHIE

This energy-boosting smoothie combines immune-boosting apricot and mango with digestion-soothing pineapple.

Preparation time: 10 minutes, plus soaking and freezing
Serves 4

3 ripe **mangoes**, peeled, pitted, and coarsely chopped
½ cup **dried apricots**
2½ cups **pineapple juice**
1 **pineapple**, peeled, cored, and chopped
finely grated zest and juice of 2 **limes**

Put the mango chunks into a freezer container and freeze overnight. Put the apricots into a bowl with the pineapple juice and chill overnight.

The next morning, put all the ingredients into a blender or food processor and blend until smooth. Serve immediately.

CHOCOLATE & ALMOND SQUARES

With fewer than 200 calories each, these satisfying snacks are full of stress-busting whole grains, nuts, and seeds.

Preparation time: 10 minutes, plus cooling and chilling
Cooking time: 20 minutes
Makes 15–20

....

finely grated zest of 1 **lemon**
½ cup chopped **dried dates**
1 cup chopped **almonds**
½ cup firmly packed **light brown sugar**
3¼ cups **millet flakes**
1½ cups **cornflakes**, lightly crushed
1⅔ cups **bran flakes**
1 (14 oz) can **condensed milk**
2 oz **dark chocolate**, melted, plus extra to drizzle (optional)
3 tablespoons **mixed seeds**, such as pumpkin, sesame, and sunflower

Put all the ingredients into a large bowl and mix together. Spoon into a 11 x 7 inch nonstick baking pan and place in a preheated oven, at 350°F, for 20 minutes.

....

Remove from the oven and let cool. Once cool, drizzle the top with melted chocolate, if desired. Mark into 15–20 squares and chill in the refrigerator until firm. Store in an airtight container in a cool place for up to a week.

....

FRUITY MANGO OAT BARS

Oat bars are the perfect snack, providing slow-release energy and keeping stress and all of its symptoms at bay.

Preparation time: 10 minutes, plus cooling
Cooking time: 30 minutes
Makes 12
················

½ cup firmly packed **light brown sugar**
1¼ sticks **butter**
2 teaspoons **light corn syrup**
2 cups **rolled oats**
4 teaspoons **mixed seeds**, such as pumpkin
  and sunflower
½ cup coarsely chopped **dried mango**

Put the sugar, butter, and syrup into a large, heavy saucepan over low heat until melted, then remove from the heat and stir in the remaining ingredients.
··

Spoon the mixture into an 11 x 7 inch nonstick baking pan, press down lightly, and place in a preheated oven, at 300°F, for 30 minutes, until golden around the edges.
··

Use a small knife to score the bake into 12 pieces, then let cool completely before removing from the pan. Cut or break into 12 pieces once cooled. Store in an airtight container for up to a week.
··

SWEET POTATO & CABBAGE SOUP

Full of fiber and antioxidants to protect against the effects of stress, this soup is also hearty and flavorsome.

Preparation time: 20 minutes
Cooking time: 25 minutes
Serves 4

2 **onions**, chopped
2 **garlic cloves**, sliced
4 **bacon** or **turkey bacon**
    strips, chopped
3 **sweet potatoes**,
    peeled and chopped
2 **parsnips**, chopped
1 teaspoon chopped **thyme**
4 cups **vegetable stock**
1 baby **savoy cabbage**, shredded
sea salt and **black pepper**
soda bread, to serve

Put the onions, garlic, and bacon in a large saucepan over medium heat and cook for 2–3 minutes. Add the sweet potatoes, parsnips, thyme, and stock, bring to a boil, and simmer for 15 minutes or until the vegetables are tender.

Remove from the heat, let cool slightly, then transfer two-thirds of the soup to a blender or food processor and blend until smooth. Return to the pan, add the cabbage, and continue to simmer for 5–7 minutes, until the cabbage is just cooked. Season to taste, ladle the soup into warm bowls, and serve with soda bread.

BACON & CANNELLINI BEAN SOUP

A filling winter soup bursting with warming flavors and low-GI beans to keep energy levels steady.

Preparation time: 15 minutes
Cooking time: 20 minutes
Serves 4
....

1 teaspoon **olive oil**
2 **smoked bacon** strips, chopped
2 **garlic cloves**, crushed
1 **celery stick**, finely chopped
1 **carrot**, finely chopped
1 **onion**, chopped
2 teaspoons **dried thyme**
finely grated zest and juice of 1 **lemon**
2 (15 oz) cans **cannellini beans**,
    drained and rinsed
4 cups **vegetable stock**
2 tablespoons chopped **parsley**
sea salt and **black pepper**
crusty **bread**, to serve

Heat the oil in a large saucepan, add the bacon, garlic, celery, carrot, and onion and cook over medium heat for 3–4 minutes, until the bacon is beginning to brown and the onion soften.
....

Add the thyme, lemon juice, and lemon zest and continue to cook for 1 minute. Add the beans and stock to the pan, bring to a boil, reduce the heat, and simmer for 10 minutes.
....

Remove from the heat, let cool slightly, then transfer the soup to a blender or food processor and blend with the parsley until smooth. Return to the pan, season to taste, and heat through. Ladle the soup into warm bowls and serve with crusty bread.
....

BROILED MUSHROOM & GARLIC WRAPS

Mushrooms are a key calming ingredient, encouraging healthy sleep and reducing the effects of stress on mind and body.

Preparation time: 20 minutes
Cooking time: 15 minutes
Serves 4
....

1 lb large **portobello mushrooms**, thickly sliced
2 **garlic cloves**, finely chopped
3 **scallions**, thinly sliced
2 tablespoons **olive oil**
½ cup **cream cheese**
4 large whole-grain soft flour **tortillas**
¼ cup chopped **chives**
12 **cherry tomatoes**, quartered
2 **romaine lettuce**, shredded
sea salt and **black pepper**

Toss the mushrooms with the garlic, scallions, and olive oil in a large bowl. Season to taste, transfer to a nonstick baking sheet, and place under a preheated medium broiler for 6–8 minutes, until tender, turning frequently.

Meanwhile, spread the cream cheese over the tortilla wraps and sprinkle with the chives. Divide the mushrooms among the wraps, sprinkle with the cherry tomatoes, and top with a handful of the lettuce. Fold up the tortillas to completely enclose the filling, creating 4 packages.

Heat a large, ridged grill pan over medium-high heat. Place the packages on the grill and toast for 4–5 minutes, turning occasionally, until nicely charred on both sides. This may need to be done in two batches. Cut in half and serve immediately with the remaining lettuce.

LEMONY SCALLOP SKEWERS WITH ARUGULA

Treat yourself to this simple, elegant lunch for a special occasion and boost your immunity at the same time.

Preparation time: 10 minutes
Cooking time: 5 minutes
Serves 4

1 lb large **scallops** without roes
finely grated zest and juice of 1 **lemon**
3 teaspoons **basil oil**
¾ cup **hazelnuts,** blanched
1 (5 oz) package **arugula**
sea salt and **black pepper**

Put the scallops into a bowl with the lemon zest and 2 teaspoons of the basil oil and season with black pepper. Mix well to coat, then thread the scallops onto 4 metal skewers.

Place the skewers under a preheated hot broiler for 2–3 minutes, until just cooked, turning occasionally. They are ready as soon as they are firm and opaque.

Meanwhile, heat a small skillet over medium heat, add the hazelnuts, and dry-roast until golden, shaking the skillet frequently. Transfer the nuts to a small dish and crush lightly.

Toss the arugula leaves with the remaining basil oil and the lemon juice and season to taste. Arrange on 4 serving plates and top with the scallop skewers. Sprinkle with the hazelnuts and serve immediately.

GREEN LENTILS WITH FLAKED SALMON

This powerful stress-busting combination of lentils and salmon will encourage relaxation and wellbeing on all levels.

Preparation time: 30 minutes
Cooking time: 25 minutes
Serves 4

1 lb **salmon tail fillet**
2 tablespoons dry **white wine**
⅔ cup **green lentils**, well rinsed
2 **red bell peppers**, halved, cored, and seeded
large handful of **dill**, chopped
finely grated zest and juice of 1 **lemon**
bunch of **scallions**, finely sliced
sea salt and **black pepper**

Dressing
2 **garlic cloves**
large handful of **flat leaf parsley**, chopped
large handful of **dill**, chopped
1 teaspoon **Dijon mustard**
2 **green chiles**, seeded and chopped
juice of 2 large **lemons**
1 tablespoon **olive oil**

Put the salmon onto a large sheet of aluminum foil and spoon the wine over the ifsh. Gather up the sides of the foil and fold over at the top to seal into a package. Put onto a baking sheet and bake in a preheated oven, at 400°F, for 15–20 minutes, until just cooked.

Place the lentils in a large saucepan with plenty of water, bring to a boil, then simmer gently for about 15–20 minutes, until cooked but still firm to the bite.

Meanwhile, place the bell peppers, skin side up, under a preheated hot broiler until charred. Place in a plastic bag for a few minutes. Remove from the bag, peel off the skin, and cut the flesh into 1 inch squares.

Put all the dressing ingredients, except the oil, into a blender or food processor and blend until smooth. With the motor still running, drizzle in the oil until the mixture is thick. Season to taste.

Drain the lentils and put into a bowl with the red bell pepper, dill, lemon zest, and most of the scallions. Season to taste and stir in the dressing. Flake the salmon and gently stir through the lentils. Squeeze lemon juice over the fish to taste and sprinkle with the remaining scallions. Serve warm or cold.

SMOKED MACKEREL PASTA SALAD

Smoked mackerel is the ultimate in convenience superfoods and provides a heart-healthy, nervous-system boosting meal in moments.

Preparation time: 15 minutes
Cooking time: 10–15 minutes
Serves 4

....

10 oz **whole-grain** or spelt **conchiglie pasta**
2 cups **green beans**, trimmed
4 **pepper-crusted smoked mackerel fillets**, skin and bones removed
4 cups **mixed peppery salad greens**
½ **cucumber**, seeded and chopped
2 **scallions**, finely sliced
2 hard-boiled **eggs**, shelled and quartered

Dressing
½ cup **reduced-fat sour cream**
1 tablespoon **whole-grain mustard**
1 teaspoon **French mustard**
2 tablespoons **lemon juice**
1 teaspoon chopped **dill**
1 teaspoon chopped **tarragon**
sea salt and **black pepper**

Cook the pasta in a large saucepan of lightly salted boiling water for 11 minutes, or according to package directions, until al dente. Drain and cool under cold running water. Transfer to a large bowl and set aside.

Meanwhile, cook the green beans in a saucepan of lightly salted boiling water for 4–5 minutes, until just tender. Drain and cool under cold running water, then add to the bowl with the pasta.

Put all the dressing ingredients into a screw-top jar, season to taste, and shake vigorously until well combined.

Flake the smoked mackerel into large pieces and stir into the pasta and beans with the salad greens, cucumber, and scallions. Toss with a little of the dressing and divide among 4 serving bowls. Top with the hard-boiled eggs and serve with the remaining dressing on the side.

ROASTED BEET & FETA SALAD WITH ALMONDS

Beet provides a powerhouse of nutrients and this warm, tasty salad will lift the mood and keep you satisfied for hours.

Preparation time: 20 minutes
Cooking time: 25 minutes
Serves 4

8 large **beets**, peeled
and cut into chunks
2 tablespoons **olive oil**
½ cup blanched **almonds**
3½ cups **arugula**
5 oz **feta cheese**
2 tablespoons **balsamic** glaze
4–5 **mint leaves**, chopped
sea salt and **black pepper**

Put the beets into a nonstick baking pan and drizzle with the olive oil. Season to taste and use your hands to toss the beets in the oil until evenly coated.

Place in a preheated oven, at 400°F, for about 25 minutes, until tender, turning once or twice. About 5 minutes before the end of cooking time, add the almonds to the pan.

Divide the arugula among 4 serving plates, top with the beets and almonds, and crumble the feta cheese over the top. Drizzle with the balsamic glaze and the oil from the baking pan.

Sprinkle with the mint and serve warm or cold. The salad can be stored in an airtight container in the refrigerator for up to 2 days.

GOAT CHEESE, APPLE & WALNUT SALAD

This fruity, filling salad is rich in protein and antioxidant nutrients to help prevent damage caused by stress.

Preparation time: 15 minutes
Cooking time: 5 minutes
Serves 4

2 **goat cheese** logs, cut
   into ½ inch slices
2 teaspoons **olive oil**
7 cups **mixed salad greens**
16 **dried apricots**, sliced
1 cup **walnuts**, lightly toasted
handful of **grapes**, halved
2 **Granny Smith apples**, peeled,
   cored, and cut into slices
sea salt and **black pepper**
whole-grain rolls, to serve

Dressing
2 tablespoons **olive oil**
2 tablespoons **lemon juice**
½ teaspoon **sea salt**
½ teaspoon **black pepper**
1 teaspoon **honey**
1 teaspoon **whole-grain mustard**

Place the goat cheese slices on a nonstick baking sheet and brush with a little olive oil. Season to taste, then place under a medium-hot broiler until bubbling. Meanwhile, put all the dressing ingredients into a screw- top jar and shake vigorously until combined.

Divide the salad greens among 4 plates and top with the apricots, walnuts, grapes, and apples. Arrange a hot goat cheese slice on top of each one and drizzle with the dressing. Serve immediately with whole-grain rolls.

WATERMELON & FETA SALAD

Watermelon is hydrating and a natural source of electrolytes, which boost energy and ease headaches and muscular tension.

Preparation time: 10 minutes
Cooking time: 2 minutes
Serves 4

1 tablespoon **black sesame seeds**
4 cups, peeled, seeded, and diced **watermelon**
1¼ cups diced **feta cheese**
2 (5 oz) packages **arugula**
large handful of **mint**, **parsley**, and **cilantro** sprigs
⅓ cup **olive oil**
1 tablespoon **orange flower water**
1½ tablespoons **lemon juice**
½ teaspoon **sugar**
1 teaspoon **pomegranate syrup** (optional)
sea salt and **black pepper**

Heat a skillet and dry-fry the sesame seeds for 2 minutes, until aromatic, then set aside. Arrange the watermelon and feta on a large plate with the arugula and herbs.

Whisk together the oil, orange flower water, lemon juice, sugar, and pomegranate syrup, if using. Season to taste, then drizzle teh dressing over the salad. Sprinkle with the sesame seeds and serve.

WARM SPINACH SALAD

Full of stress-busting superfoods, this salad is ideal for lunch or as an appetizer or side dish for dinner.

Preparation time: 15 minutes
Cooking time: 10 minutes
Serves 4

....

1 teaspoon **olive oil**
4 **turkey bacon** strips
1 **garlic clove**, crushed
1 **shallot**, finely chopped
3 tablespoons **sherry vinegar**
2 lb **spinach**, washed and dried
4 hard-boiled **eggs**, shelled and sliced
8 large **mushrooms**, thinly sliced
1 **avocado**, peeled, pitted, and diced
sea salt and **black pepper**

Heat the olive oil in a large nonstick skillet and add the bacon. Cook until crisp, then remove with a slotted spoon and drain on paper towels. Add the garlic and shallot to the skillet and sauté gently for 3–4 minutes.

....

Stir in the vinegar and season to taste. Turn off the heat and add the spinach. Toss it gently in the dressing until just covered and beginning to wilt. Divide the spinach among 4 serving plates and top with the eggs, mushrooms, bacon, and avocado. Serve immediately.

....

GINGERED TOFU & MANGO SALAD

The soy in the tofu is a good hormone balancer and source of energy. Here, it is combined with stress-busting mango.

Preparation time: 15 minutes
Cooking time: 5 minutes
Serves 4
....

8 oz **tofu**
1½ inch piece fresh **ginger root**, peeled and grated
¼ cup **light soy sauce**
2 **garlic cloves**, crushed
2 tablespoons seasoned **rice vinegar**
¼ cup **peanut oil**
2 bunches of **scallions**, diagonally sliced
1 cup **cashew nuts**
2 small **mangoes**, peeled, pitted, and sliced
1 small **iceberg lettuce**, shredded
¼ cup **water**

Pat the tofu dry on paper towels and cut into ½ inch cubes. Mix the ginger, soy sauce, garlic, and vinegar in a bowl, add the tofu, and toss to coat. Set aside to marinate for 15 minutes.
....

Remove the tofu from the marinade and reserve the marinade. Heat the oil in a skillet over medium heat, add the tofu, and cook gently for about 3 minutes, until golden. Remove from the pan and keep warm.
....

Add the scallions and cashews to the skillet and cook quickly for 30 seconds. Add the mango slices and cook for another 30 seconds, until heated through.
....

Pile the lettuce onto serving plates and sprinkle the tofu, scallions, mango, and cashews over the top. Heat the marinade juices in the pan with the measured water, pour the mixture over the salad, and serve immediately.
....

MEDITERRANEAN BROWN RICE SALAD

The vibrant colors pay tribute to the antioxidants in this salad. Add crumbled feta or a few pine nuts before serving, if you like.

Preparation time: 25 minutes
Cooking time: 30–40 minutes
Serves 4

2 **red bell peppers**, cored, seeded, and chopped
2 **yellow bell peppers**, cored, seeded, and chopped
2 large **zucchini**, cubed
4 small **beets**, peeled and cubed
1 large **eggplant**, cubed
1 large **onion**, coarsely chopped
3 tablespoons **olive oil**
2 teaspoons **dried oregano**
4 cups cooked **brown rice**
sea salt and **black pepper**
5 **basil leaves**, torn, to garnish

Dressing
1 tablespoon **olive oil**
1 teaspoon **honey**
1 teaspoon **dry mustard**
½ teaspoon **salt**
½ teaspoon **black pepper**
1 teaspoon **dried oregano**
2 tablespoons **balsamic vinegar**

Arrange the vegetables on 2 nonstick baking pans and drizzle with the olive oil. Season to taste, sprinkle with the oregano, and use your hands to toss the vegetables in the oil until evenly coated.

Place in a preheated oven, at 400°F, for 30–40 minutes, until tender and just beginning to brown at the edges, turning once or twice.

Transfer the vegetables to a serving bowl with a slotted spoon and set aside. Put all the dressing ingredients into a screw-top jar, season to taste, add the oil from the baking pans, and shake vigorously until well combined.

Place the cooked rice and dressing in the bowl with the vegetables and toss together until well mixed. Serve warm or cold, garnished with the basil. The salad can be stored in an airtight container in the refrigerator for up to 5 days.

TURKEY, PEANUT & MANGO SALAD

This is a wonderfully fragrant, nutritious lunch. Use the freshest mango you can find for optimum antioxidant protection.

Preparation time: 15 minutes
Serves 4

....

1 (1 lb) package **mixed salad greens**
1 lb cooked **turkey** or **chicken**,
 light and dark meat
12 **cherry tomatoes,** halved
1 **mango**, peeled, pitted, and cut into chunks
⅔ cup roasted **peanuts**
3 cups chopped fresh **cilantro**

Dressing
3 tablespoons **olive oil**
2 tablespoons **lime juice**
finely grated zest of ½ **lime**
2 teaspoons packed **brown sugar**
2 teaspoons **Thai fish sauce**
½ teaspoon **sweet chili sauce**

Put the salad greens on a large plate and arrange the turkey, cherry tomatoes, and mango on top. Sprinkle with the roasted peanuts and cilantro.

....

Put all the dressing ingredients into a screw-top jar and shake vigorously until well combined. Pour over the salad, lightly toss, and serve.

....

WILD RICE & TURKEY SALAD

Wild rice isn't a rice at all, but a hearty, wholesome grain that has all the benefits of whole grains.

Preparation time: 10 minutes, plus cooling
Cooking time: 30 minutes
Serves 4

1¾ cups **wild rice**
2 **green apples**, quartered,
    cored, and finely sliced
¾ cup **pecans**
finely grated zest and juice of 2 **oranges**
⅔ cup **cranberries**
3 tablespoons **olive oil**
2 tablespoons chopped **parsley**
4 **turkey breast cutlets**, about 4 oz each
sea salt and **black pepper**

Cook the rice according to package directions and let cool. Mix the apples into the rice with the pecans, orange zest, orange juice, and cranberries. Season to taste.

Mix together the oil and parsley and season to taste. Cut the turkey cutlets into halves or thirds lengthwise and coat with this mixture.

Heat a skillet until it is hot but not smoking and cook the turkey for 2 minutes on each side, until cooked through. Slice the turkey and serve immediately with the rice salad.

GRILLED TURKEY SANDWICH

The tryptophan-rich turkey in this lower-calorie grilled sandwich encourages relaxation, while the spinach balances energy levels.

Preparation time: 10 minutes
Cooking time: 8–10 minutes
Serves 4

8 slices of **whole-grain bread**
3 tablespoons **whole-grain mustard**
1¾ cups shredded **Gruyère** or **reduced-fat cheddar** or **American cheese**
8 oz cooked **turkey**, thinly sliced
2 **tomatoes**, sliced
2 **scallions**, thinly sliced
¼ cup **low-fat cream cheese** (optional)
1 tablespoon **vinegar**
4 extra-large **eggs**
3½ cups **baby spinach**
sea salt and **black pepper**
chopped **chives**, to garnish

Lay 4 slices of the bread on a board and spread with the mustard. Top with half the shredded cheese, the turkey, and tomato slices, then sprinkle with the scallions. Season to taste and sprinkle with the remaining shredded cheese.

Spread the cream cheese, if using, over the remaining slices of bread and place, cheese side down, on top of the sandwiches.

Heat a large, nonstick skillet over medium heat until hot, then carefully add the sandwiches and cook for 4–5 minutes or until golden and crispy. This may need to be done in two batches. Turn the sandwiches over and cook for another 4–5 minutes.

Meanwhile, bring a large saucepan of water to a gentle simmer and add the vinegar. Carefully break 2 eggs into the water and cook for 3 minutes. Remove with a slotted spoon and keep warm. Repeat with the remaining eggs.

Place the sandwiches on serving plates, sprinkle with the spinach, and top each with a poached egg. Garnish with chives and serve immediately.

FISH & MANGO CURRY WITH BROWN RICE

This Thai-inspired dish is quick and nutritious. Use halibut, red snapper, or Alaskan pollock—or chicken or shrimp, if you prefer.

Preparation time: 20 minutes
Cooking time: 20 minutes
Serves 4

2 tablespoons **olive oil**
3½ cups **coconut milk**
1½ lb firm **white fish fillets**, cut into chunks
1 large **mango**, peeled and cut into chunks

Curry paste
2 in piece of fresh **ginger root**,
   peeled and chopped
finely grated zest and juice of 2 **limes**
2 small **green chiles**, seeded
3 **lemon grass stalks**, outer leaves removed
4 **shallots**, peeled
3 cups fresh **cilantro**
4 **garlic cloves**
1 teaspoon **sea salt**
3 tablespoons **Thai fish sauce**

To serve
brown rice
1 cup fresh **cilantro**, roughly torn

Put all the curry paste ingredients into a food processor or mini chopper and blend until smooth, adding a little water if it is too dry to make a paste.

Heat the oil in a nonstick skillet or wok, add the curry paste, and cook gently for 2–3 minutes. Add the coconut milk and cook, covered, for 5 minutes. Add the fish, stir gently, and continue to cook for another 5 minutes.

Stir in the mango and cook, uncovered, for 3–4 minutes, until the fish is flaky and the mango heated through. Serve with brown rice and a generous sprinkling of cilantro.

SALMON WITH MASHED BEANS & CELERIAC

With omega-rich salmon and high-quality protein in the beans, this dish will calm, relax, and aid a good night's sleep.

Preparation time: 15 minutes
Cooking time: 20 minutes
Serves 4

½ head of **celeriac**, cut into chunks
2 potatoes **potatoes**, cut into chunks
1 cup cooked **edamame (soybeans)**
3 tablespoons **water**
4 **salmon fillets**, about 4 oz each
3 tablespoons **butter**
3 tablespoons chopped **chives**
3 tablespoons chopped **tarragon** or **dill**
1 tablespoon **white wine vinegar**
sea salt and **black pepper**

Cook the celeriac and potatoes in a saucepan of lightly salted boiling water for about 15 minutes, until tender. Put the beans and measured water into a blender or food processor and blend until smooth.

Meanwhile, pat the salmon fillets dry on paper towels and season to taste. Heat 1 tablespoon of the butter in a skillet and cook the salmon for 4–5 minutes on each side, until just cooked through.

Drain the vegetables and return them to the pan with the blended beans and another 1 tablespoon of the butter. Using a potato masher, mash together the ingredients until evenly combined. Reheat for 1–2 minutes and season to taste.

Pile the mashed beans and vegetables onto 4 warm serving plates and top with the salmon fillets. Add the remaining butter, herbs, and vinegar to the skillet and heat through until the mixture bubbles. Pour the sauce over the salmon and serve immediately.

SPICY SHRIMP KEBABS WITH WILD RICE

A great source of zinc for memory, energy, and libido, these spicy shrimp kebabs are delicious and quick to prepare.

Preparation time: 10 minutes
Cooking time: 5 minutes
Serves 4

....

24 fresh peeled **jumbo shrimp**
½ cup **sweet chili sauce**
finely grated zest and juice of 2 **limes**
¼ cup **light soy sauce**
1 tablespoon **sesame oil**
sea salt and **black pepper**

To serve
wild rice
crunchy **green salad**

Thread the shrimp onto 4 metal skewers, running the skewers through the shrimp in 2 or 3 places to secure. Whisk together the chili sauce, lime zest, lime juice, soy sauce, and sesame oil, and brush on both sizes of the shrimp.

....

Place under a preheated hot broiler and cook for 1–2 minutes on each side until pink and just cooked through. Serve with wild rice and a crunchy green salad.

....

THAI MUSSEL CURRY WITH GINGER

This fragrant, light curry provides a good boost of zinc, encouraging energy and even supporting a flagging libido.

Preparation time: 30 minutes
Cooking time: 15 minutes
Serves 4

3 lb **mussels**
1 tablespoon **sunflower oil**
1¾ cups **reduced-fat coconut milk**
4–5 **kaffir lime leaves**
⅔ cup **fish stock**
2 teaspoons **Thai fish sauce**

Curry paste
½ –1 large **red chile** halved and seeded
2 **shallots**, peeled
1 **lemon grass stalk**, outer leaves removed finely grated zest and juice of 1 **lime**
1½ inch piece of fresh **ginger root**, peeled and chopped

To serve
2 cups fresh **cilantro**, coarsely torn
brown rice

To prepare the mussels, remove any barnacles with a small knife and pull off the hairy beards. Rinse the shells well and discard any mussels that are open or have broken shells. Put them in a bowl of clean water until ready to cook.

Place all the curry paste ingredients in a food processor or mini chopper and blend until smooth, adding a little water if it is too dry to make a paste.

Heat the oil in a nonstick skillet or wok, add the curry paste, and cook gently for 5 minutes. Add the coconut milk, kaffir lime leaves, fish stock, and fish sauce and cook for 3 minutes.

Drain the mussels and add to the pan. Cover and cook for about 5 minutes, until the mussel shells have opened. Divide among 4 warm bowls, discarding any mussels that have not opened. Sprinkle the cilantro over the top and serve with brown rice.

ROOT VEGETABLE STEW WITH POMEGRANATE SALSA

This fragrant Moroccan tagine, or stew, contains a medley of stress-busting herbs, spices, and root vegetables.

Preparation time: 25 minutes
Cooking time: 1 hour
Serves 6–8

1 **cinnamon stick**
½ teaspoon **cloves**
½ teaspoon **cardamom seeds**
2 teaspoons **coriander seeds**
1 teaspoon **ground turmeric**
1 tablespoon **olive oil**
1 large **onion**, chopped
1 inch piece of fresh **ginger root**, peeled and grated
3 **garlic cloves**, finely chopped
½ **red chile**, seeded and chopped
2 (14½ oz) cans diced **tomatoes**
1 large **carrot**, cubed
1 **sweet potato**, cubed
½ **butternut squash**, cubed
3½ cups **spinach**
1 (15 oz) can **chickpeas**, rinsed and drained
handful of fresh **cilantro**, chopped
1 teaspoon **harissa**
quinoa, to serve

Pomegranate salsa
seeds from 1 **pomegranate**
2 **scallions**, finely chopped
juice of 1 **lime**
10–12 **mint leaves**, finely chopped
1 tablespoon **olive oil**

Dry-fry the cinnamon, cloves, cardamom, and coriander seeds in a skillet until their fragrance is released. Use a mortar and pestle or a clean coffee gzester to grind them to a powder with the turmeric.

Heat the olive oil in a large, heavy saucepan and stir in the spices. Add the onion and cook for 2–3 minutes, then add the ginger, garlic, and chile. Reduce the heat and cook gently for 10 minutes, until soft.

Add the tomatoes, carrot, sweet potatoes, and squash, cover, and simmer for 30–40 minutes, until the vegetables are tender.

Stir the spinach, chickpeas, cilantro, and harissa into the stew, season to taste with salt and black pepper, cover, and set aside.

Make the pomegranate salsa by mixing together all the ingredients. Serve the tagine on a bed of quinoa with the salsa on the side.

GINGERY CHICKPEA CURRY

This quick curry provides plenty of protein to encourage stable blood sugar levels and promote healing.

Preparation time: 15 minutes
Cooking time: 40 minutes
Serves 4

....

1 tablespoon **olive oil**
2 **garlic cloves**, crushed
2 **onions**, chopped
3 in piece of fresh **ginger root**,
    grated, plus extra to serve
1 teaspoon **mild chili powder**
1 teaspoon **ground cumin**
½ teaspoon **ground coriander**
½ teaspoon **ground turmeric**
½ teaspoon **sea salt**
½ teaspoon **garam masala**, plus extra
    to serve
2 (15 oz) cans **chickpeas**,
    rinsed and drained
1¾ cups **coconut milk**
3 cups chopped fresh **cilantro**
black pepper
quinoa or **brown rice**, to serve

Heat the oil in a deep saucepan or wok over medium heat and add the garlic, onions, and ginger. Cook slowly, stirring often, until the onions are soft and beginning to caramelize.

....

Add the chili powder, cumin, ground coriander, turmeric, sea salt, and garam masala and cook for another 2–3 minutes. Add the chickpeas and coconut milk, stir well, cover, and simmer for 20 minutes.

....

Remove the lid and continue to cook for another 10 minutes, mashing some of the chickpeas into the sauce to thicken. Season with pepper, sprinkle with a pinch of garam masala, a grating of fresh ginger, and the fresh cilantro and serve immediately with quinoa or brown rice.

....

POTATO & ONION TORTILLA

Keep the skin on the potatoes to add extra fiber to this surprisingly light tortilla and add a handful of grated Gruyère, if desired.

Preparation time: 10 minutes
Cooking time: 30 minutes
Serves 6

6 red-skinned or white round **potatoes**, thinly sliced
¼ cup **olive oil**
2 large **onions**, thinly sliced
6 **eggs**
2 teaspoons **dried thyme**
1 teaspoon **dried rosemary**
sea salt and **black pepper**

Put the potatoes into a bowl and toss with a little seasoning. Heat the oil in a heavy ovenproof skillet, add the potatoes, and cook gently for 10 minutes, turning frequently, until softened but not browned.

Add the onions and cook gently for another 5 minutes without browning. Spread the potatoes and onions in an even layer in the pan and turn the heat down as low as possible.

Beat the eggs in a bowl with the herbs and season to taste. Pour the eggs into the pan, cover, and cook gently for about 15 minutes, until the eggs have set.

If the center of the omelet is still liquid, place the pan under a preheated moderate broiler to finish cooking. Transfer the tortilla to a plate and serve warm or cold.

WILD MUSHROOM STROGANOFF & MASHED SWEET POTATOES

The creamy calming mushroom stroganoff is counterbalanced by the antioxidant-rich sweet potatoes.

Preparation time: 15 minutes
Cooking time: 20 minutes
Serves 4

2 tablespoons **butter**
1 tablespoon **olive oil**
1 **onion**, sliced
12 ounces **cremini mushrooms**, sliced
2 **garlic cloves**, finely chopped
2 teaspoons **paprika**, plus extra to garnish
⅓ cup **vodka**
1¾ cups **vegetable stock**
generous pinch of **ground cinnamon**
generous pinch of **ground mace**
5 oz **wild mushrooms**, sliced if large
⅓ cup **crème fraîche**
sea salt and **black pepper**
chopped **parsley**, to garnish

Mashed sweet potatoes
3 large **sweet potatoes**, peeled and cubed
2 tablespoons **crème fraîche**
1 teaspoon grated **nutmeg**

Cook the sweet potatoes in a saucepan of lightly salted boiling water for 15–20 minutes, or until tender. Drain, season to taste, and mash with the crème fraîche and nutmeg.

Meanwhile, heat the butter and oil in a skillet, add the onion, and cook for 5 minutes, until lightly browned. Stir in the cremini mushrooms and garlic and cook for 4 minutes, until tender. Stir in the paprika and cook for another 1 minute.

Pour in the vodka. When it is bubbling, flame with a match and stand well back. Once the flames have subsided, stir in the stock, cinnamon, and mace and season to taste. Simmer for 3–4 minutes.

Add the wild mushrooms and cook for 2 minutes or until tender, then stir in 2 tablespoons of the crème fraîche. Divide among 4 serving plates, top with the remaining crème fraîche, and garnish with a sprinkling of paprika and a little parsley. Serve with the mashed sweet potatoes.

BAKED SWEET POTATOES WITH VEGETABLE CHILI

This is an easy, filling dish designed to satisfy and calm. The chili freezes well and can also be served in warm corn tortillas.

Preparation time: 20 minutes
Cooking time: about 40 minutes
Serves 4

....

2 tablespoons **olive oil**
1 large **onion**, chopped
½ **butternut squash**, peeled and cubed
1 teaspoon **cayenne pepper**
1 teaspoon **ground cumin**
1 teaspoon **ground cinnamon**
2 **red bell peppers**, cored, seeded, and chopped
1 **zucchini**, cubed
1 **red chile** seeded and finely sliced
1 **green chile** seeded and finely sliced
3 **garlic cloves**, finely sliced
1 (15 oz) can **chickpeas**, rinsed and drained
1 (15 oz) can **red kidney beans**, rinsed and drained
2 (14½ oz) cans diced **tomatoes**
large bunch of fresh **cilantro**
4 **sweet potatoes**, scrubbed
sea salt and **black pepper**
½ cup **sour cream**, to serve

Heat the oil in a large saucepan and add the onion. Cook for about 10 minutes over medium heat until golden and caramelized. Add the squash, cayenne pepper, cumin, and cinnamon and season to taste. Cook for 1-2 minutes.

....

Add the bell peppers, zucchini, chiles, and garlic and cook for another 3-4 minutes. Add the chickpeas, beans, and tomatoes and the stems from the bunch of cilantro.

....

Meanwhile, prick the sweet potatoes all over with a fork and place in a preheated oven, at 400°F, for 20-30 minutes, or until cooked all the way through.

....

Simmer the chile covered, for about 25 minutes, until the sauce is thick and the vegetables tender, adding a little water if it becomes too dry. Season to taste, sprinkle with the cilantro leaves, and serve with the baked sweet potatoes topped with the sour cream.

....

TURKEY BURGERS
WITH SWEET POTATO WEDGES

This is a family-friendly meal for a relaxing evening in.
The tryptophan-rich turkey ensures a good night's sleep.

Preparation time: 20 minutes
Cooking time: 30–40 minutes
Serves 4

1 lb ground **turkey**
2 **scallions**, finely chopped
2 teaspoons **dried tarragon**
½ teaspoon **sea salt**
½ teaspoon **black pepper**
1 **egg**, lightly beaten
4 **whole-wheat buns**
4 large slices of **tomato**
4 **lettuce leaves**

Sweet potato wedges
4 large **sweet potatoes**, peeled
    and cut into wedges
1 tablespoon **olive oil**, plus extra
    for greasing
1 teaspoon **paprika**
½ teaspoon **sea salt**
½ teaspoon **black pepper**

Use your hands to toss together all
the ingredients for the sweet potato
wedges in a large bowl, then arrange
on a greased baking sheet. Place on
the top shelf of a preheated oven,
at 400°F, for 30–40 minutes, or until
golden and crisp.

Meanwhile, mix the turkey with the
scallions, tarragon, salt and black pepper,
then stir in the egg until well combined.
Use your hands to shape the mixture into
4 large balls, then press them firmly into
patty shapes.

Place under a preheated hot broiler
for about 8 minutes on each side,
or until golden and cooked through.
Serve each burger in a whole-wheat
bun, with a slice of tomato and lettuce,
and sweet potato wedges on the side.

HERBED QUINOA WITH LEMON & CHICKEN

Quinoa is rich in omega oils that boost brain power and nourish the nervous system. What's more, it is delicious.

Preparation time: 15 minutes
Cooking time: 15 minutes
Serves 4

1¼ cups **quinoa**
1 tablespoon **olive oil**
1 **onion**, chopped
1 **garlic clove**, crushed
1 lb skinless, boneless **chicken breasts**, sliced
1 teaspoon **ground coriander**
½ teaspoon **ground cumin**
⅓ cup **dried cranberries**
½ cup chopped **dried apricots**
¼ cup chopped **parsley**
¼ cup chopped **mint**
finely grated zest of 1 **lemon**
sea salt and **black pepper**

Cook the quinoa in a saucepan of lightly salted boiling water for 15 minutes, until tender, then drain.

Meanwhile, heat the oil in a large skillet, add the onion, and cook for 5 minutes, until softened. Add the garlic, chicken, coriander, and cumin and cook for another 8–10 minutes, until the chicken is cooked through.

Add the chicken mixture, cranberries, apricots, herbs, and lemon zest to the quinoa and season to taste. Stir well and serve warm or cold.

CHICKEN & BARLEY RISOTTO

Barley is a wonderfully nutritious grain that works well in this light risotto, offering a good hit of the calming B vitamins.

Preparation time: 10 minutes
Cooking time: 40 minutes
Serves 4

....

4 cups **chicken stock**
2 tablespoons **olive oil**
1 large **onion**, finely chopped
10 oz mixed **mushrooms**
2 **garlic cloves**, crushed
1 cup **pearl barley**
10 oz **asparagus**, trimmed and chopped
1½ cups cubed cooked **chicken**
½ cup grated **Parmesan cheese**
finely grated zest of 1 **lemon**
sea salt and **black pepper**

Heat the stock in a saucepan until it reaches simmering point, and let it continue simmering while you cook.

Heat the olive oil in a large saucepan or skillet and add the onion. Cook gently for 5–10 minutes, until soft, then stir in the mushrooms and garlic. Turn up the heat and cook for 4–5 minutes, until tender.

Add the barley and a ladleful of hot stock and cook gently, stirring continuously, until the stock has all but been absorbed. Add another ladleful of stock and repeat until only about 2 ladlefuls of stock remain in the saucepan.

Add the asparagus and chicken to the remaining stock in the saucepan and simmer for 2–3 minutes while you continue to stir the risotto.

Add the remaining stock, asparagus, and chicken to the risotto and cook until the barley is tender and all of the liquid has been absorbed. Stir in the Parmesan cheese and lemon zest, season to taste, and serve immediately.

LAMB & BEAN STEW

Lamb is an excellent source of iron and beans help sustain energy levels, making sure you feel full for hours.

Preparation time: 15 minutes
Cooking time: 1 hour 25 minutes
Serves 4

1 teaspoon **olive oil**
12 oz **lean lamb**, cubed
16 small **shallots**, peeled
1 **garlic clove**, crushed
1 tablespoon **all-purpose flour**
2½ cups **lamb stock**
¾ cup canned diced **tomatoes**
1 **bouquet garni**
2 (15 oz) cans **great Northern beans,**
    rinsed and drained
12 **cherry tomatoes**
sea salt and **black pepper**
brown rice or **green beans**, to serve

Heat the oil in a large saucepan over medium-high heat, add the lamb, and cook for 3–4 minutes, until browned all over. Remove from the pan and set aside.

Reduce the heat, add the shallots and garlic to the pan, and cook gently for 4–5 minutes, until softened and just beginning to brown.

Return the lamb and any juices to the pan, stir in the flour, and add the stock, tomatoes, bouquet garni, and beans. Bring to a boil, stirring, then cover and simmer for 1 hour, until the lamb is just tender.

Add the cherry tomatoes and season to taste. Continue to simmer for 10 minutes, then serve with brown rice or green beans.

MANGO BRÛLÉE

This delicious, warming dessert provides a host of key nutrients, including yogurt to calm and encourage healthy digestion.

Preparation time: 10 minutes
Cooking time: 5 minutes
Serves 4
....

2 large, ripe **mangoes**, peeled, stoned and sliced
2 teaspoons **rum** or 2 teaspoons **vanilla extract**
1 teaspoon **ground cinnamon**
1½ cups **live Greek yogurt**
6 teaspoons **brown sugar**

Divide the sliced mango between 4 small ovenproof dishes, filling them about half way, then drizzle with the rum or vanilla, and sprinkle with the cinnamon.
....

Spoon the yogurt over the mango and smooth to level. Sprinkle with the brown sugar then place under a preheated medium grill for about 5 minutes, until the sugar begins to bubble and caramelize. Serve immediately.
....

BLUEBERRY & LEMON ICE CREAM

Blueberries help balance weight and ease anxiety.
This refreshing ice cream can be enjoyed any time.

Preparation time: 10 minutes, plus freezing
Serves 4
....

2 cups **frozen blueberries**
2 cups **live Greek yogurt**
1 cup **confectioner's sugar**,
    plus extra to decorate
finely grated zest and juice of 2 **lemons**

Set aside a few blueberries for decoration.
Place the remaining blueberries in a blender
or food processor with the yogurt, icing
sugar and lemon zest and juice and blend
until smooth.
....

Spoon the mixture into a 3-cup freezerproof
container and freeze until softly frozen and
easily spoonable. Before serving, decorate
with the reserved blueberries and a
sprinkling of confectioner's sugar.
....

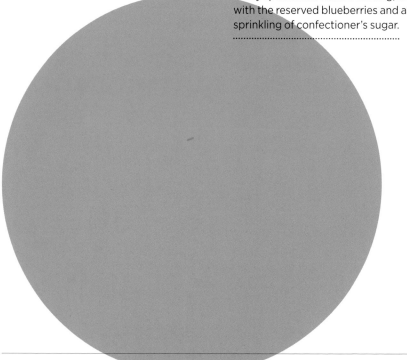

BAKED BANANAS

Bananas contain multiple stress-busting nutrients so this delicious dessert is the perfect way to end a stressful day.

Preparation time: 15 minutes
Cooking time: 20 minutes
Serves 4

....

4 large firm **bananas**
2 teaspoons **brown sugar**
1 teaspoon **vanilla extract**
1 teaspoon **maple syrup**
1½ teaspoons **butter**
handful of **almonds**
   or **pistachios**, chopped (optional)
live Greek yogurt, to serve

Make a long slit down the centre of each of the unpeeled bananas. Place each banana, cut-side up, in the centre of a large piece of foil.

....

Mix together sugar, vanilla, maple syrup and butter, and spoon into the slits in the bananas. Wrap carefully in the foil, ensuring that the bananas remain upright with the slits at the top.

....

Place in a preheated oven, 400°F, for 20 minutes. Open the parcels, sprinkle with the nuts, if using, and serve immediately with Greek yogurt.

....

BROWN RICE PUDDING

Brown rice gives this creamy pudding a nutty flavor and a hit of stress-busting nutrients.

Preparation time: 10 minutes
Cooking time: about 1¾ hours
Serves 4
....

1⅓ cups **heavy cream**,
   oat cream or soya cream
1¼ cups **water**
½ cup **brown rice**
½ cup **golden raisins**, **raisins**
   or **dried cranberries**
3 **egg yolks**
3 teaspoons **demerara sugar**
1 teaspoon **ground cinnamon**
2 teaspoons **vanilla extract**
1 teaspoon **butter**, melted

Place the cream, measured water and rice in a large, heavy saucepan over medium heat and stir well. Bring to a boil, then reduce the heat to a simmer and cook for about 1½ hours, stirring regularly, until the rice is tender and all of the liquid has been absorbed. Add a little more water if it starts to dry out.
....

Stir in the dried fruit and cook for another 10 minutes, until plump, stirring frequently.
....

Mix the egg yolks, sugar, cinnamon, vanilla and butter in a small bowl, then add to the rice mixture and cook over a gentle heat for about 5 minutes, stirring constantly, until it thickens. Remove from the heat and serve immediately.
....

CRANBERRY & APPLE CRISP

This is a great winter warmer with a crunchy, nutty topping, rich in healthy oils and soothing oats.

Preparation time: 20 minutes
Cooking time: 30 minutes
Serves 4

4 **Granny Smith apples**, peeled, cored, and finely sliced
2 teaspoons **cornstarch**
2 teaspoons **ground cinnamon**
4 teaspoons **honey**
1 cup **fresh** or ⅔ cup **dried cranberries**
finely grated zest and juice of 1 **orange**
Greek yogurt with live active cultures, to serve

Topping
2 cups **rolled oats**
2 teaspoons **ground cinnamon**
½ cup **almonds**, crushed
½ cup **brazil nuts**, crushed
2 drops of **vanilla extract**
2 teaspoons **butter**, melted, plus extra for dotting

Put the apples in a large bowl and stir in the cornstarch, cinnamon, honey, and cranberries until coated, then add the orange juice and orange zest. Transfer the mixture to an ovenproof dish and press down lightly.

Mix together all the topping ingredients, then press on top of the apple and cranberry mixture and dot with a little extra butter.

Place in a preheated oven, at 400°F, for 30 minutes, or until the topping is golden and the apple juices are starting to bubble at the edges of the dish. Serve hot with yogurt.

CHERRY & CINNAMON PARFAIT

Cinnamon boosts immunity, stabilizes blood sugar, encourages brain function, and reduces levels of cortisol.

Preparation time: 10 minutes, plus cooling and freezing
Cooking time: 5 minutes
Serves 4

....

2 cups **Morello cherries** in syrup
1 tablespoon **ground cinnamon**
1 teaspoon **vanilla extract**
1 teaspoon **sugar**
1 **egg yolk**
⅔ cup **reduced-fat crème fraîche** or **Greek yogurt**
4 **meringue nests**, broken into pieces
fresh cherries, to decorate

Drain the cherries and measure ½ cup of the syrup into a small saucepan. Stir in the cinnamon, vanilla, and sugar and heat for 5 minutes or until the sugar has dissolved. Set aside to cool.

....

Mix the egg yolk and crème fraîche. Add the drained cherries to the syrup, then stir in the crème fraîche and egg. Fold the crushed meringue carefully through the mixture.

....

Transfer to a 1½-cup freezerproof container and freeze for at least 4 hours. Eat within a day, when the parfait will be softly frozen. Decorate with fresh cherries before serving.

....

RICOTTA, PLUM & ALMOND CAKE

Plums and almonds are a wonderful combination. This nutritious cake makes a wonderful dessert or snack, rich in omega oils.

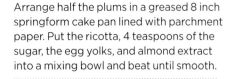

Preparation time: 20 minutes,
 plus cooling and chilling
Cooking time: 35 minutes
Serves 6
....

butter, for greasing
8 **sweet red plums**, quartered and pitted
1 cup **ricotta cheese**
4-5 teaspoons packed **light brown sugar**
3 **eggs**, separated
¼ teaspoon **almond extract**
4 teaspoons **slivered almonds**
2 teaspoons **water**
1 teaspoon **confectioners' sugar**, sifted,
 to serve

Arrange half the plums in a greased 8 inch springform cake pan lined with parchment paper. Put the ricotta, 4 teaspoons of the sugar, the egg yolks, and almond extract into a mixing bowl and beat until smooth.
....

Whisk the egg whites in a clean bowl until stiff peaks form. Carefully fold into the ricotta mixture, then spoon the mixture over the plums.
....

Sprinkle the top with the slivered almonds and place in a preheated oven, at 325°F, for 30-35 minutes, until the cake is well risen, golden brown, and the center is just set. Cover the top loosely with aluminum foil after 20 minutes if it is browning too quickly.
....

Turn off the oven and let the cake cool for 15 minutes with the door slightly ajar. Cool completely, then chill in the refrigerator.
....

Meanwhile, cook the remaining plums with the measured water in a covered saucepan for 5 minutes. Remove from the heat, cool slightly, then blend until smooth in a blender or food processor. Taste and add the remaining sugar, if necessary.
....

Transfer the cake to a serving plate. Dust the top with the confectioners' sugar and serve, cut into wedges, with the plum sauce.
....

BLUEBERRY WHIP

You'll get a big hit of antioxidant-rich blueberries in this creamy dessert, which takes only minutes to make.

Preparation time: 5 minutes
Serves 4

2 cups **blueberries**
5 teaspoons **honey**
2 teaspoons **lime juice**
8 **mint leaves**
½ cup store-bought **low-fat vanilla pudding**
1 cup **Greek yogurt with live active cultures**
4 teaspoons finely chopped unsalted **pistachios**

Put the blueberries, honey, lime juice, and half the mint leaves into a blender or food processor and blend until smooth.

Add the pudding and yogurt and blend again to combine. Spoon into individual glasses, sprinkle with the pistachios, and top with the remaining mint leaves before serving.

RASPBERRY YOGURT GRATIN

Bursting with antioxidants and digestion-boosting yogurt with live cultures, this is one dessert with surprisingly few calories.

Preparation time: 5 minutes, plus cooling
Cooking time: 5-6 minutes
Serves 4

4 cups **raspberries**
1½ cups **Greek yogurt with live active cultures**
2 teaspoons **vanilla extract**
1 teaspoon **cassis** or **black currant syrup**
2 teaspoons packed **light brown sugar**

Put the raspberries in a shallow, ovenproof dish. Beat the yogurt with the vanilla and cassis or syrup, then spoon over the raspberries and level the surface.

Sprinkle the brown sugar evenly over the top, then place under a preheated hot broiler for 5-6 minutes, until the sugar starts to caramelize. Cool slightly then serve.

DARK CHOCOLATE FONDUE WITH FRUIT & NUTS

This is a decadent, mood-boosting treat, which is elegant enough to serve at a dinner party.

Preparation time: 5 minutes
Cooking time: 10 minutes
Serves 4
....

4 oz **semisweet dark chocolate**
1 teaspoon **salted butter**
1 teaspoon **vanilla extract**
2 teaspoons **plain yogurt with
     live active cultures**

To dip
brazil nuts
almonds
dried apricots
grapes
cherries

Melt the chocolate in a heatproof bowl over a saucepan of gently simmering water, making sure the water does not touch the bottom of the bowl. Stir until melted and shiny.
....

Add the butter, vanilla, and yogurt and stir until well combined. Remove from the heat and serve immediately, with the nuts and fruit for dipping.
....

SOUR CHERRY CHOCOLATE BROWNIE CAKES

Sour cherries, which provide a host of emotional and physical benefits, are teamed here with sweet, rich chocolate.

Preparation time: 15 minutes
Cooking time: 15 minutes
Serves 4

6 tablespoons **unsalted butter**, softened, plus extra for greasing
½ cup firmly packed **light brown sugar**
1 teaspoon **vanilla extract**
¼ cup unsweetened **cocoa powder**, sifted
⅓ cup **all-purpose flour**, sifted
¼ teaspoon **baking powder**
1 **egg**
⅓ cup **dried sour cherries**
heavy cream or **crème fraîche**, to serve

Place the butter, sugar, and vanilla in a bowl and beat with a handheld electric mixer until light and fluffy. Add the cocoa, flour, baking powder, and egg and mix until combined, then stir in the cherries.

Spoon the batter into 4 cups of a lightly greased 6-section nonstick muffin pan and place in a preheated oven, at 350°F, for 10–12 minutes or until just cooked but still soft in the centers.

Turn out the desserts onto 4 serving plates and serve immediately with heavy cream or crème fraîche.

RESOURCES

American Foundation for Suicide Prevention
Tel: (888) 333)AFSP (toll-free)
Tel: (212) 363-3500 (local)
E-mail: inquiry@afsp.org
Web site: www.afsp.org

American Meditation Society
Tel: (877) 747-4267
Web site: www.americanmeditationsociety.org

American Society for Nutrition
Tel: (301) 634-7050
Web site: www.nutrition.org

Anxiety and Depression Association of America
Tel: (240) 485-1001
Web site: www.adaa.org

Black Women's Health Imperative
Tel: (202) 548-4000
E-mail: info@BlackWomensHealth.org
Web site: www.blackwomenshealth.org

Depression and Bipolar Support Alliance
Tel: (800) 826-3632 (toll-free)
E-mail: info@dbsalliance.org
Web site: www.dbsalliance.org

Food and Nutrition Information Center
Tel: (301) 504-5414
E-mail: FNIC@ars.usda.gov
Web site: fnic.nal.usda.gov

Freedom From Fear
Tel: (718) 351-1717 ext. 19
E-mail: help@freedomfromfear.org
Web site: www.freedomfromfear.org

Mental Health America
Tel: (800) 969-6642 (toll-free)
Tel: (703) 684-7722 (local)
Web site: www.mentalhealthamerica.net

National Alliance on Mental Illness
Tel: (800) 950-6264 (toll-free)
Tel: (703) 524-7600 (local)
Web site: www.nami.org

National Eating Disorders Association
Tel: (800) 931-2237 (toll-free)
Tel: (206) 382-3587 (local)
E-mail: info@NationalEatingDisorders.org
Web site: www.nationaleatingdisorders.org

National Institute of Mental Health
Tel: (866) 615-6464 (toll-free)
Tel: (301) 443-4513 (local)
E-mail: nimhinfo@nih.gov
Web site: www.nimh.nih.gov/index.shtml

National Women's Health Network
Tel: (202) 682-2640
E-mail: healthquestion@nwhn.org
Web site: nwhn.org

North American Menopause Society
Tel: (800) 774-5342 (toll-free)
Tel: (440) 442-7550 (local)
E-mail: info@menopause.org
Web site: www.menopause.org

North American Vegetarian Society
Tel: (518) 568-7970
Web site: www.navs-online.org

Postpartum Support International
Tel: (800) 944-4PPD (toll-free)
tel: (503) 894-9453 (local)
Web site: www.postpartum.net

Society for Nutrition Education and Behavior
Tel: (800) 235-6690 (toll-free)
Tel: (317) 328-4627 (local
E-mail: info@sne.org
Web site: www.sne.org

INDEX

Acknowledgments

Gill Paul would like to thank the very talented team at Octopus: Denise Bates, who came up with the idea for the series; Katy Denny, Alex Stetter, and Jo Wilson who edited the books so efficiently and made it all work; and to the design team of Jonathan Christie and Isabel de Cordova for making it all look so gorgeous. Thank you also to Karel Bata for all the support and for eating my cooking.

Karen Sullivan would like to thank Cole, Luke, and Marcus.

Picture credits